Myth

Memory grows
dim as we age.

Truth

As we grow older,
we actually add-on
more mental abilities.

...yth

There is a 'best time'
for learning.

Truth

The clock has
nothing to do with
remembering.

This is one of those rare books that can help
all of us with something that is both troublesome and
worrisome – our memory. It does this with ease, not
by attempting to teach some exhausting rote-memory
techniques, but in 12 easy and effortlessly smooth steps.

Shakuntala Devi's down-to-earth writing and encouraging
step-by-step approach puts super memory in reach of
everyone. As she says, 'Take my word. You can start
applying my memory-enhancing techniques immediately,
right now. Before you will realize, applying my methods
and strategies will become your second nature.'

Shakuntala Devi has been honing and teaching her memory
improvement techniques for more than 40 years. *Super
Memory* is the result of her life's work, specially tailored to
our needs as we age, and encompassing all of the many
ways we can use a better memory every day.

The Author

Born to an orthodox Brahmin family in Bangalore, Shakuntala Devi manifested an extraordinary love for numbers at a very early age. By the time she was five years old she had become an expert in complex mental arithmetic. The rest, as they say, is now history. Problems that took learned men hours to solve, she could solve in seconds; she could out-speed and out-calculate the fastest of computers. Put to test in the UK, her admirers and critics alike were left in daze by her mental abilities. BBC called it a 'mind-collapsing' proof of her mental abilities, and hailed her as an authentic heroine of the twentieth century.

An ardent proponent of the infinite capabilities of the human mind, she regularly conducts seminars and workshops on 'mind dynamics' in which she demonstrates and teaches techniques for developing the latent potential of human mind, including a range of memory honing techniques. The feed-back from these workshops has been enormous, and this book, *Super Memory*, is born out of her intense desire to help each of us to benefit from the brain-power we possess.

She has authored several international bestsellers which have sold millions of copies worldwide and have been translated into many languages. She is also the recipient of Ramanujan Mathematical Genius Award, which was bestowed on her in Washington, USA, in 1988.

SUPER
MEMORY
IT CAN BE YOURS!

SHAKUNTALA DEVI

Orient
Publishing
DELHI | MUMBAI | HYDERABAD

ISBN : 978-81-222-0507-7

Super Memory: It Can be Yours

Subject: Self-Help

© Shakuntala Devi

1st Published 2011
18th Printing 2016

Published by
Orient Publishing
(an imprint of Orient Paperbacks)
5A/8 Ansari Road, New Delhi-110 002
www.orientpublishing.com

Design by Vision Studio

Printed at
Yash Printographics, Noida

Printed on Chlorine-free eco-friendly paper.

Contents

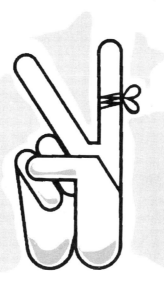

Introduction

For months I had been mentally lobbing around the idea of a memory-improvement book that could be pursued in the privacy of a student's home, at a time best suited to him or her. The germ of the idea had been implanted in my mind by several students who had attended my memory-development workshops. They wanted me to write a book that they could keep as a permanent reference and refresher. It set those mental wheels churning. Sounded like a good idea, I thought.

The idea was cemented by another student. She hugged me spontaneously after a session. 'You've changed the way I look at myself!' she exclaimed. 'I feel I'm brimming over with confidence ... as if I've added on more grey cells in my brain! I feel now as if ... I could ... take on the world!'

Click! The writer in me responded wholly. I *would* write this book!

But ... easier said than done! There I was, pen clutched in anticipation in my hand, my eyes staring at a piece of blank paper for an hour. But there were more questions than answers jostling for attention in my mind. To whom should I address this book? Should I limit its scope to a refresher series for those who had attended my memory-improvement workshops? Or should I reach out to anyone who wanted to optimise his powers of memorisation and concentration? And if so, what should my approach be? What exactly did I wish to communicate?

The mail delivered the answer! Shalan, a close friend and an author and journalist herself, had sent me a short story she'd written in the sci-fi genre. She thought (she wrote), it would interest me because it had to do with ... I won't explain it. Instead, I'll be a little unconventional and, with her permission, reproduce the story for you. I think you'll enjoy the fine ironies it spells out ...

✂ ✂ ✂

2044 by Shalan Savur

Some things don't change. You'd think that in the year 2004 things would be different from 1944 or 1844 or 1744 or even as far back as 44 or 4. To think that once man crawled on all fours. But that was in the days when The Great Artist Himself was still in the planning stages, or so Darwin would lead us to believe.

But then, Man surprised the Great Artist when he suddenly stood on two feet and found he still had two more (later called hands) to eat with, throw with, fight with. It produced the strangest results as you can see.

As Man's head rose higher, so did his ideas. From the humble bullock-cart, he graduated to the automobile and then to the aeroplane until, finally, he designed the rocket. By then, his head was well into the clouds and it's no wonder that he desired to reach the moon.

The Great Artist was ecstatic. Ah, the marvel he had produced had no limit. He called that extra special thingummy inside Man's brain: Intelligence. But all this was, as you know, in the years 4 and 44 and perhaps even up to 1944.

But, remember; we are in the year 2044. Until then the Great Artist was pleased, for Man offered Him his prayers in the simplest, if not the quaintest, of ways. He knelt, he bowed, he folded his hands, he lit candles, *diyas*, *agarbattis*. But things took a different turn.

Man devised the computer. It began by doing simple little calculations. It added, subtracted, multiplied, divided. But as the years passed by, Man added on more and more ideas to make the computer's simple little insides into a complex labyrinth-like network.

So it came to pass that, by the year 2044, the computer had taken over completely. It had (and you must believe this when I say it) Intelligence. Of course, Man patted himself for his progress. Now, he had a machine that ate, drank, played sport, waged wars, and even thought for him.

Indeed, the Great Artist felt a little uncomfortable to have the prayers faxed to Him. It was strange to see Man reclining on his easy-do-all chair and languidly blow on a button to send up those precious prayers. It was even more strange to see electronic *agarbattis* come on like psychedelic lights.

I've said earlier, things hadn't changed in 2044. It is just that the methods had become easier. But the Great Artist's great mind was in great turmoil. And well it would be. What had happened to that marvel called Man that He had created?

His muscles were shrinking due to lack of use. Ditto his brain power for ditto reasons. The whole world was being run from a keyboard by robots. The Great Artist could see the great world that he had designed from a big bang of inspiration shrink and shrivel in front of His great eyes. Would it disappear with a whimper?

So, the Great Artist sat down for a great think. Then, he called all the natural elements to His aid. The wind, the water, the sunshine, all of which Man had tried to tame but thankfully had not succeeded.

'Go forth,' He commanded. 'And knock some sense into Man's head. But don't hurt him.'

'I'll blow hot and cold,' said the wind, for the great lung-power of the earth had regretfully picked up Man's jargon.

'I'll swim against the tide,' said the water, 'and have a whale of a time.'

'I'll serve man days sunny-side down,' said the sunshine.

The Great Artist watched with great anxiety the happenings of 2044. It was a devastation which even Nostradamus hadn't foreseen. The wind whirled and twirled things out of shape. The water tidal-waved continents from east to west, north to south, and sometimes even north-west or south-east or south-west. The sun disappeared for days on end, playing a skilful game of hide-and-seek.

The computers which had been fed with set data and fixed formulae now threw out confused signals. Breakfast-shows became dinner-shows. The weather computer threw up its antenna in despair.

As for Man, he didn't know whether he was standing on his feet or on his head. So to save himself he went down on all fours.

Here, with his ears on the ground, he thought long and hard. He had seen the Stone Age, the Bronze Age, the Iron Age, the Steel Age, the Golden Age, the Jet Age, the Supersonic Age, the Jazz Age, the Space Age. Not necessarily in that order, for you must remember his brains were a trifle scrambled. He concluded that this was the Confused Computer Age.

He tried to stand on his two feet, but his weakened muscles didn't allow him to. He tried to think, but his rusted brain didn't allow him to. He tried to pray, but he had forgotten how to. Indeed, he thought that the world had come to an end and waited in dread for the final shudder that would send him plummeting down the big black hole of the Universe.

But it didn't happen.

For the Great Artist watched over him with great anxiety. And as the earth righted itself Man stood up once again and vowed that he would never let himself grow slack and useless. And the Great Artist rejoiced greatly. And all this happened in 2044.

⚔ ⚔ ⚔

I chuckled. Unwittingly, Shalan had set the course for my book. Most sci-fi writers focus on the war between artificial intelligence and human genius. Man versus power-hungry machine. But it took that special Indian mind to go beyond the master-slave dystopia, and point to the 'Great Artist' within and without us who could make his own course corrections and set the balance right.

And, of course, Shalan's perception melds so smoothly with the New Age think — that we should evolve to a higher level of consciousness. A plane in which the technology we produce will also alter its emphasis and will be directed more at feeding the soul than indulging the collective ego, where science will work towards achieving a balance rather than controlling the world with its death-dealing weapons. For, science must liberate man rather than dehumanising him, must be the source of continuing aliveness for the sustenance of the human spirit. All this means, of course, that we must transform ourselves in order to transform the machines that we make to transform our world.

Now I could see it so lucidly. Man is in danger of losing the potency of his God-given faculties — by taking them for granted even as he blindly pursues and allows himself to be driven by crafted artificiality. In the hands of man, Science should be a strong, tensile string that unreels smoothly, allowing man's Intelligence to soar and to garner wisdom from the whispers of information and knowledge blowing in the free and open skies of life. Man should never allow that Intelligence to be snagged — like Charlie Brown's kite — and then to be shredded and scattered to the winds like lost thoughts.

Human memory is one of our primary intellectual faculties. Today, in a world of files and floppies and discs that can store reams of information and reproduce them at will, we tend to forget all too easily that human memory is not merely the repository of information in the brain. It is much more than this, and something that a machine can never be: a *power*, a *force* by which we mentally reproduce not just information but also our experiences, by which we shape our perceptions, introspect, interpret and analyse the direction our life has taken. Thanks to our memory, we can not only reproduce knowledge but also *apply* it to avoid past pitfalls and to steer a better course in the future.

Memory is also the force that affirms our very identity. Example: Sheetal remembers every morning, that she is Sheetal. It is her memory that enables her to associate her life's experiences with her identity as Sheetal. If she hadn't been blessed with a memory, if instead, when she awoke, a computerised monitor blinked out the words, GOOD MORNING! YOU ARE SHEETAL!, she would be no better than a programmed robot!

The memory force ensconced and nurtured in our subconscious is the eternally-awake, joyous, higher self within us. It is an implanted chip that our spirit recognises and rejoices in as an affirmation of our higher intelligence — what priests refer to as 'the soul ever living in God'. For some, memory even serves as the bud of immortality. Nurtured and cultivated, it enables them to recall not only the events of this life but also of past lives!

Memory integrates our self (or personhood) with culture, civilisation, modernity, country, the world. It can motivate us to great achievements, to supreme endeavours. When Rabindranath Tagore started his revolutionary, open-air educational institution, he said, 'I know what it is to which this school owes its origin. It is not to any new theory of education, but to the memory of my schooldays.' His memory linked two experiences — 'our regular type of school ... a manufactory specially designed for grinding out uniform results' and 'our family (that) lived in the freedom of ideas ... It made us fearless in our freedom of mind ... This was the education I had in my early days, freedom and joy in the exercise of my mental and artistic faculties.' And a living experiment called *Shanti Niketan* was born.

This is what I want this book to do for you: release the immense power of your memory so that you can dream and link events and experiences and take off on that joyous flight of spirit where you are free, aloft. From those liberating heights, life will appear vital, unfettered, effortlessly smooth. And that's where and how you'll want to stay for the rest of your life — in the open skies, breathing fresh breezes, attuned to your own links of self-discovery.

This book blooms from the inspired land of the *Bharatvasis*, named not only after the legendary King Bharat, but also for the wisdom of its spiritual intellectuals who lived up to their names — for *bha* means 'to shine'. It's there in our *smritis* — our memories.

Chapter **1**

YES, YOU CAN...

Unjam the mind blocks
that cause you to forget

Double your powers
of concentration

Learn to develop an open mind

Banish those myths
about memory

TOOLS YOU'LL USE

Memory Foods

Sunshine 'n' Fresh Air

Fun 'n' Games

Sleeping 'n' Dreaming

Exercise

Positive Thinking

AND YOU WILL...

Permanently shift gears
from, 'I have a terrible
memory ...' to, 'I can
remember anything
that I want to...'

Get Set For An 'Unforgettable' Experience!

How to prepare your mind for its most
exciting and challenging adventure ever

A friend of mine, whom I was expecting to drop in at 11 one morning, made it only by three in the afternoon. Her explanation: 'When I sat in the bus, my mind suddenly went blank. I couldn't tell the conductor where I wanted to get off because I couldn't remember it myself. So he punched a ticket to the last stop. I got off, but I felt disoriented. So fogged, in fact, that I even forgot my name.' She stood at the bus-stop till her memory returned. Then she caught the next bus to her destination and rang my door-bell, four hours late!

My friend's temporary bout of total amnesia is not explained in terms of ageing brain cells or a congenitally deficient memory. My friend was an unhappy woman, under severe mental and financial strain. Her husband was suffering from a progressive, incurable disease. Her emotional ordeal was compounded by the sheer practical demands of caring for him. Yet, after a bracing cup of hot tea and a bowl of *upma*, there she was, sitting and laughing and joking with me. Nobody would have imagined that, just a few hours before, her hopelessness and turmoil had clouded her mind so oppressively that it had blanked out memory.

'Poor memory' has been blamed on all kinds of suspects ('I just wasn't born smart', 'Age is catching up with me'), but the fact is that the most common culprits are the least suspected ones. Unhappiness, for instance. It can usher in the dark, heavy clouds of fear, anger and resentment that overturn your mental equilibrium and blotch out memory. Most memory experts fail to give due importance to mental tranquility. Yet, in its absence, you might be able to train your brain to remember better temporarily, but you will not be able to make remembering a lifelong habit. It's when you possess inner calm that you are able to retain your sense of reason, your sense of balance, your sense of humour. In this state of rational tranquility, you operate from a basis of fact, not sentiment. And facts are what memory is all about.

A robust memory requires fertile ground on which to thrive. Not only a clear mind, but other pre-requisites go into its making. So, before we get down to the actual techniques for improving memory, let us make sure that we prepare well the soil in which it is to be nurtured. Start with these important preliminary strategies before you go on to the next chapter; without them you will not derive the full worth of this book.

Throw Out the Mental Clutter

Let's suppose that a month or so ago, you read the word, 'screever', looked up its meaning in the dictionary and filed away the information for future retrieval. Today you're trying to recall that word, but for some unfathomable reason, it eludes you. Why?

One reason could be the mental blocks that are jamming the highway of your mind. Negative emotions are one of the impediments that can impede clear traffic. As the *Bhagvad Gita* says, '... From anger results delusion, from delusion results confusion of memory ...' Not only anger, but a scroll of other unhappy emotions can fog your mind: fear, depression, self-pity, envy, grief, hatred, restlessness, anxiety. With this mist overhanging your mind, your senses can get dulled to the point where you are not registering even your immediate environment or experiences. Thus, you may:

- Pass a friend on the street, look at him, but *do not see* him.
- Listen to someone who's talking to you, but *do not hear* her or later recall a single word she said.
- Touch a snake in the wild undergrowth, but *do not feel* it.
- Eat a delicious meal served to you, but *do not taste* it, or later even remember what it was you ate!
- Inhale the gas leaking from your cylinder, but *do not register its smell* — with potentially disastrous consequences.

Make a conscious effort to weed out negative thoughts from your mind, to send it positive, harmonious messages. The great sage, Paramahansa Yogananda, asks us to remind ourselves every day: *'I am a prince(ss) of peace, sitting on the throne of poise, directing my kingdom of activity.'* Memorise this sentence. Say it to yourself when you awaken each morning. Repeat it to yourself whenever you find yourself in a situation that threatens to upturn your mental equilibrium. Until, gradually, you find that equilibrium is more and more easily acquired and that finally it gets embedded as a natural feature of your thoughtscape.

Once this happens, you won't find yourself turning into a mass of quivering jelly with a bad case of exam nerves or interview fright. The mental equilibrium you've instilled in yourself will still those butterflies in your stomach: All you'll need to do is take a deep breath and tell yourself with confidence, 'It will all come back to me in a minute.' And it will!

Keep an Open Mind

Let me illustrate the importance of this with a riddle which I would like you to try and solve. It was set by the mind wizard, Harry Lorayne: 'Here is the Roman numeral IX. Can you add just one mark or symbol to this Roman numeral, and change it into the number 6?'

If you have a closed mind, you'll rack your brain and never come up with the answer. Or you will give up immediately from disinterest. In case you haven't been able to solve Lorayne's riddle, here is the answer: 'Simply add an "S" in front of the letters IX and you've formed the word "SIX"!'

See what I mean? Your memory knows IX and S and SIX. But it's only if you're open-minded that you can bridge these separate memory strands, link them together and come up with a new concept.

When you allow yourself to get stuck in a mental groove, you put the brakes on your imagination and interest, limiting your ability to build bridges to memories, to link a present problem to past information and to arrive at a solution or a new idea.

Open-mindedness was precisely the route by which Newton, watching an apple fall to the ground, arrived at the laws of gravity. And Archimedes, looking at the water overflow from

his bath-tub when he was immersed in it, gave the world Archimedes' principle. If these two men of science had not had that memory-link ticking in their brilliant brains, they might never have given the world those Eureka findings. Which is why I say: keep an open mind!

To do that, you'll need to force your brain out of its old, well-worn grooves by keeping yourself creatively challenged. Try things like designing a new wardrobe for yourself (even if you never actually go out and buy up all those clothes and accessories), reading a book on an unfamiliar subject or dreaming up 10 innovative uses for a paper clip. You've got to *exercise* your mind to make it more flexible.

Rev Up Your Powers of Concentration

If your attention is not focused, you will not fully absorb a piece of learning or other task on hand; and if you do not absorb, you cannot retain. But what most people do not realise is that concentration is really a matter of habit. You can learn a score of mental exercises to improve your concentration, but if you do not transfer these principles to your day-to-day functioning and give them the underpinnings of a habit, there will be no lasting impact on your powers of concentration.

Before I continue, let me explain the difference between being preoccupied and concentrating.

Preoccupation is a kind of mental teasing game, with worry nibbling at your thoughts and scattering them in several directions so that you are unable to think clearly.

Concentrating, on the other hand, means harnessing your mental forces and bringing a bull's-eye centering of attention to a particular task. Researchers have found that this state, which they call 'flow', seems to calm down the cerebral cortex (where the memory centre is located). This brings a feeling of relaxed alertness. There is a loss of self-consciousness. Aches go unnoticed, background noises unheard. As distinct from preoccupation, concentration has such positive factors as willpower and commitment attached to it.

One of the chief things running interference with concentration are those internal pollutants we've talked about before: anger, fear, doubts and distractions. These can replace concentration with restless preoccupation and mental turmoil. I have already talked about the importance of cultivating the positive attitude that will help drive out defeatist thoughts. Optimism optimises memory.

Another concentration trip-up is the pressure of several tasks demanding your attention. My advice in such a situation is: Prioritise. Put the most urgent task on the front burner and have the other jobs queue up behind it in order of importance. Then tackle each task with verve, going from one to the next, with an occasional breather in between.

The 'verve factor' is extremely important. It means giving each task your absolute attention, bringing to it what I call 'work meditation' — becoming one with your work. It also means that you should not care about the result. As the *Bhagvad Gita* says: 'He who does the prescribed work without caring for its fruit is a *sanyasi*.' If you don't allow your mind to be distracted by thoughts of what you're going to gain from this work, you'll be able to bring conviction and commitment to the work at hand. And that translates into powerful concentration.

Concentration can sometimes become difficult if an assignment appears overwhelming. In this case, try breaking down the assignment into more 'do-able' tasks. If you have to research a report, write it up and present it, make the researching a goal in itself. Once that's done, the second step, outlining it, becomes easier. Writing it up becomes your third goal; and then, finally, focus on the final step: presenting your findings.

Broken down into four manageable chunks, it becomes easier for each one to be pursued with effortless concentration.

Concentration dispels chaos and brings in order. And who can deny that from an organised mind emerges a powerful memory?

Take it Easy!

Many mnemonic experts have devised clever tricks involving a lot of mental acrobatics, some so complicated that it is more difficult to learn the tricks than just to remember what you wanted to in the first place! Thus, if you're struggling through a complex course and trying to apply one of these very convoluted methods to it, you might just decide to give up! Or, your mind will become so saturated and fatigued with the strain of learning that you may end up feeling like a zombie. Worse, you might even persuade yourself that you're dumb!

Rest assured, this book will not have you floundering in deep waters. Which is why my first bit of advice to you if you wish to power up your memory is to R-E-L-A-X! Don't be in a tearing hurry to become a human computer. The fact is: Relaxation will do your memory more good than frenzied haste. When you're relaxed, your mind is far more receptive. When you're relaxed, you're sending silent, positive messages to your self. That you trust yourself. That you're not questioning your potential, but giving it space to expand.

Remember, you're not using this book to prove anything to anybody — only to unleash your memory potential to its maximum. So there is no need to put yourself under any 'pressure to perform'.

Take a moment right now to check out how relaxed you are. Are your lips pursed, your temples drawn, your forehead creased? Are your shoulders hunched and tense? Stop right there! Loosen those muscles, stretch those limbs, shrug your shoulders before you read on.

Practise relaxation techniques in the course of your day-to-day routine: they provide a natural antidote to the stress response. There are many routes to relaxation. One of the best is deep breathing. Breathing deeply creates an aura of relaxed awareness — the perfect mental ambience in which to give yourself positive suggestions: I *will* do better; I *can* remember anything I want.

Now and then, try some *lyming*. That's Caribbean for doing nothing — guilt-free. It gives your brain time to process information that it has received while you were in overload.

Music, playing with children, watching a movie... all these can help you shift gears from 'revved-up' to 'relaxed'. But watch it with that old tube. Relaxing occasionally before a TV programme is one thing; becoming a TV junkie is another. Too much television trains the attention to be passive and dull. Even a nuclear physicist, if he spends excessive hours watching *Baywatch*, could very well experience brain drain.

Check your Diet

The right diet is one of the essentials of good memory. If you don't eat properly, you don't nourish the brain. It's as simple as that. Just as petrol fuels your car, glucose fuels your brain. When glucose is in deficient supply, the brain begins to perform poorly.

In providing the brain with its fuel, glucose, the body seems to have a special need for vitamins of the B-complex group. They act

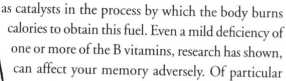

as catalysts in the process by which the body burns calories to obtain this fuel. Even a mild deficiency of one or more of the B vitamins, research has shown, can affect your memory adversely. Of particular importance are vitamins B_1 (thiamine), B_3 (niacin or nicotinic acid), Vitamin B_6 (pyridoxine), folate and vitamin B_{12} (cyanocobalamin).

Besides this role, the B vitamins are also involved in the production of chemicals needed by the brain cells to pass on messages along their nerve pathways. Thus, B_1, B_{12}, and most particularly choline, are involved in the production of acetylcholine, one of the brain's major chemical messengers. Many of the foods touted as 'brain foods' — fish, liver and eggs — contain choline. Its brain-boosting benefit has been documented not only in mice but also in humans. Research has shown a 'measurable' memory-improving effect in young, healthy adults fed on choline-rich lecithin, and the 'slower' the subject to start with, the more pronounced the effects of choline on their powers of recall.

But if there were a contest for the most promising nutrient for brain function, many researchers believe the prize might be awarded to vitamin B6. Studies have found that, in rats as well as in humans, the dendrites — branches of brain cells that carry electrical impulses from one cell to another — tend to shrivel up and die when deprived of B6. The result: a breakdown in brain circuitry. Dutch researchers who studied healthy men in their 70s found that, at the end of three months, those who had been put on a daily regimen of B6 performed better on tests of long-term memories than a control group who received a placebo (a look-alike pill).

Iron also plays an important role in maintaining alertness. The brain needs large amounts of oxygen to function effectively — 20 to 30 times more than other parts of the body — and the only way it can get it is through iron-packed red blood cells. Some researchers also think that iron influences chemicals and pathways that are involved in 'turning the brain on', so to speak. In other words, in maintaining alertness.

Studies have shown that children with iron-deficiency anemia have short attention spans and problems with new learning; they have also shown that boosting iron intake reverses these problems. Other research shows that adults too have problems with alertness and recall when their iron levels are in the 'low but normal range.'

A ready reckoner of the kind of foods you need to include in your daily diet to maintain alertness and boost memory is given on pages 28-29.

But it's not just specific nutrients like B vitamins or iron that are crucial to alertness and recall. People who have a poor diet in general are the most likely to get into trouble. Crash dieting or skipping meals can make you light-headed and poorly-focused.

Remember, though, that *balance* is the key. Overeating makes your brain sluggish and lazy. You know how lethargic you can feel after a grand celebratory feast. That's because, after a large meal, more blood is shunted to the digestive tract than to the brain. Your mind will function better if you ensure that there is a steady supply of glucose in your bloodstream, and you can do this by eating moderate portions spaced out over four to six meals a day.

Take care to avoid an overabundance of fats (oils, butter, *ghee, vanaspati,* cream); these clog the blood vessels that supply the brain, cutting down on blood flow to the brain and impeding its functioning.

Memory Foods: A Ready Reckoner

Nutrient	Reverses
Vitamin B$_1$	Memory impairment due to fatigue, nervousness or poor uptake of glucose by the brain
Vitamin B$_6$	Long-term memory reverses due to malfunctioning in the brain's circuitry
Vitamin B$_{12}$	Memory impairment due to depression, headaches and nervous disorders
Vitamin C	Memory impairment by aiding iron absorption
Iron	Memory impairment by oxygenating the brain and by influencing brain chemicals that promote alertness

Sources

Cereals: Rice bran, wheat, barley, maize, bajra.
Pulses: Peas, soyabeans, bengal, green, black & red gram, moth.
Vegetables: Lotus stems, capsicum, turnip & beet greens, colocasia & radish leaves, potatoes.
Fruits: Apricots, pineapples, bael, melon.
Meat & Poultry: Liver, sheep, muttons, eggs.
Nuts and oilseeds. Milk and milk products.

Cereals: Brown rice, wheat, barley. *Pulses:* Soya beans.
Vegetables: spinach, potatoes, cauliflower, sweet potatoes.
Fruits: walnuts, bananas, avocados, prunes, raisins. *Nuts and oilseeds.*

Fish, Meat and Poultry: Fish, shrimps, sheep, liver, goat, egg yolk, mutton.
Milk and milk products.

Cereals & Pulses: red gram, peas, maize, bengal gram.
Vegetables: parsley, drumstick leaves, turnip greens, cabbage, bitter gourd, radish leaves, carrot leaves, brussels sprouts, beet greens, celery leaves, cauliflower, fenugreek leaves, cluster beans, turnips, bathua leaves, tomatoes green, spinach, french beans, sweet potatoes, round gourds, potatoes, ladies fingers, brinjals.
Fruits: papayas, lettuce, coconuts, Indian gooseberries, guavas, oranges, limes, papayas, strawberries, lemons, pineapples, custard apples, lychees, raspberries, melon, mangoes, pomegranates.
Fish and meat. Milk and milk products.

Cereals: Rice, bajra, wheat, jowar, soya beans.
Pulses: Bengal gram, moth beans, cowpeas, peas, kidney beans, green gram.
Vegetables: lotus stems, cauliflower greens, turnip greens, colacasia leaves.
Fruits: currants, melons, raisins, dates, apricots, custard apples.
Fish and meat. Milk and milk products. Nuts and oilseeds.

Check your Alcohol Intake

Excessive long-term drinking can create vitamin deficiencies (in particular, vitamin B_1) that ultimately result in memory impairment. Alcoholics who develop a B_1 deficiency have problems with short-term memory. They may remember in detail that little watering-hole round the corner from where they lived 10 years ago, but not what they had for dinner the previous night.

In addition, alcohol itself can be toxic to the brain.

Get into that Sun

The brain isn't nourished by food alone. If you're sitting in a cramped position in a windowless room with no fresh air, you're not going to be able to concentrate or memorise well because your brain isn't getting enough oxygen. Go outside occasionally and bask in bright light. Like plants, humans, too, get a powerful surge of energy from sunlight. Spending 5 or 10 minutes in the sunshine can make a tremendous difference in your mood and stress level.

Muscle Up your Memory

If you get the feeling, more and more often, that you 'just can't think straight', check to see whether you're sitting up straight! Poor posture can put a crimp on the blood supply to your brain. And years of allowing your upper body to sag can create kinks in the spine that squeeze the two arteries passing through the spinal column to the brain, causing an inadequate blood supply. The result? Fuzzy thinking and forgetfulness, especially as you age.

But don't sit around too much — even if you're sitting up

straight. You've got to get moving, too! A growing body of evidence suggests that people who are aerobically fit may also have an edge intellectually. Researchers in this area are convinced that exercise can help improve concentration, creativity and problem-solving abilities. How? During aerobic exercise, when the heart is pumping hard, blood flow to the brain is increased and that changes the biochemistry of the brain. There's an increase in its oxygen supply.

In one study of adults in their 40s, those who took part in a ten-week walking/jogging programme beat a group of sedentary people hands down in the time it took them to respond on a test of numbers both groups had been asked to remember.

Another study showed that elderly people put on a four-month walking programme improved on six out of eight mental-ability tests, including short-term memory. The sedentary group showed no improvement.

Brisk walking is the kind of aerobic exercise that most people are comfortable with, even 'senior citizens'. Other aerobic options include: jogging, running, swimming, working out on a treadmill or on an exercycle. Choose the one that you think you're likely to stick with, or choose more than one if you prefer variety. Just do it!

Get Good Medical Care

Mental functioning, including memory, are adversely affected by certain chronic illnesses. Among them: heart disease (which can impede blood supply to the brain), diabetes, and depression (which can cause transient memory impairment). By keeping these ailments under control with good medical care, you can avoid their mind-fuzzying effects.

Think you Can — and You Will

Constantly telling yourself that you have a memory like a sieve is one perfectly good way to sabotage your true intellectual potential. Such negative thoughts keep you from pursuing knowledge and from learning better ways to remember. *And*, they can become a self-fulfilling prophecy.

Feeling good about your ability to learn is one of the first things you'll need to work at if you want to improve your memory. If you've been boffing yourself on the head with the conviction that you are lousy at learning, remember what mind trainers know so well: you really have a lot more brain than you think, and you *can* learn to use more of it than you ever thought possible.

Crush These Memory Myths

Myth : There Is A 'Best Time' for Learning
Truth : The Clock Has Nothing
        To Do With Remembering

Strange theories about memory and learning are constantly being thrown up. Some experts tell you that if you're a deep night-sleeper and a light-morning sleeper, your best times for learning are the one or two hours immediately after you awaken. And that, conversely, if you're a light night-sleeper and a deep morning-sleeper, your best learning times are afternoons or evenings. Then again, there are the 'naturalists' who insist that 6 a.m. to 11 a.m. is optimal time for short-term memory, and that 3 p.m. to 6 p.m. is the best time slot for long-term memory.

Such theories, if you take them seriously, put you in a mental strait-jacket. Both, before and after Edison, man has been defying the capricious limitations that Nature's rhythms supposedly put on him. To believe that your capacity for learning is restricted to set hours or times of the day is a preposterous notion. The truth is that the clock has nothing to do with remembering. If you lay the groundwork for a keen memory with the steps I've outlined above, you can be an ATM (Any Time Memory) member lifelong. Every second, every minute, every hour, every day can have you seeking knowledge, absorbing, remembering. On the other hand, even if you're a light morning-sleeper, but on waking up fill your mind with emotional clutter, your memory will suffer.

So, don't get yourself stuck in a time warp. Remember, anytime is memory time!

Myth : Memory Dims as We Grow Older
Truth : As We Grow Older We Actually
Add-on More Mental Abilities

One of the most persistent and destructive myths we've built up is that our memory stays good only until middle age; after that we say it's *pfft*! And I say, 'Balderdash!' You already know that you are blessed with an Any Time Memory ability. Now let me introduce you to the Any Age Memory concept.

Though we do begin to lose brain cells from around age 30, researchers at Southern California's Gerontology Centre have discovered this is simply due to disuse. The more recent findings show that around 10,000 million cells are constantly maturing, and that the millions of glia cells that connect and feed the brain cells *increase* as the brain matures.

Translated into practical terms, what this means

is that not only do we not lose the ability to remember as we grow older, we actually add on *more* mental abilities — the ability to analyse in greater depth, the ability to grasp more and to understand better.

Why, then, do I keep meeting people in their 40s, 50s and 60s, who seem hell-bent on 'preparing to age gracefully?' With resigned good humour, they say, 'It's inevitable', and proceed to start 'forgetting' things, which in turn just reinforces their belief that their memory is not what it used to be.

The truth is that your memory will not dim unless you *allow* it to slip into decline through sheer neglect. This neglect generally stems from two factors:

The Wrong Attitude. The earlier findings that brain cells decrease in number with age led to a hopelessly negative attitude among midlifers — a fatalistic belief about 'memory decline' that caused a vicious cycle to set in. Because they took it for granted that they were doomed to increasing forgetfulness, they passively allowed their mental faculties to slide into a slump. The more they allowed this to happen, the more fuzzy and forgetful they actually became. This tendency continues among most older folk today. Add to this the rigidity and inflexibility that many carry as extra baggage as they age, and what you get is atrophy.

Yet, long before the new findings about the self-renewal process in the brain, there were people who refused to become victims of a self-defeatist attitude. Two of them were Sir Winston Churchill and Rabindranath Tagore, who took up a new hobby, painting, at an age when most others have retired into a cocoon of their own creation. Then there's that oft-related gem about Associate Justice Oliver Wendell Holmes of the U.S. Supreme Court. At the age of 90, he re-read Plato, he said, 'to improve my mind!' I have no doubt that he grasped its wisdom far more than when he'd read it at 20, 30, or whenever — *and* that he remembered the context better than he ever did earlier!

Closer to our times, there have been public figures who, well into their 70s and later, continued to make their living by keeping their memories and their wits intact. At age 80 plus, actor Walter Matthau keeps up regular mind-stretching workouts. 'I read a lot, listen to music (which I find mentally stimulating) and walk about five miles a day, observing people and things. I still think of myself as 21...'

So, make time for those mental workouts. Treat your mind as a muscle. For it's certainly true that if you don't use it, you'll lose it!

A Faulty Lifestyle. This is the second culprit that can cramp our memory skills as we grow older. For most of us, studying is a process to be engaged in only until we take up a job. After that, we become so preoccupied with promotions, perquisites, acquisitions, marriage and children that we neglect both body and mind. We give physical exercise the go-bye and fall into mental lethargy. This slothful lifestyle is anathema to mental alertness and a razor-sharp memory.

The landmark Seattle Longitudinal Study, started in 1956, found that intellectual decline is very largely a matter of whether people let their minds loaf or kept them busy. One out of four 80-year-olds, for example, were as bright as they'd always been, the study found. 'There are very few toddling millionaires,' reported the study's leader, K. Warner Schaie, who is now director of the Gerontology Center at Pennsylvania State University. Also, bridge players continued to do very well on mental tests as they aged; not so bingo players. Crossword puzzle aficionados continued to do better on verbal skills, and jigsaw puzzle players tended to maintain their spatial skills.

Couch potatoes, on the other hand, were found to be the

quickest to slip into intellectual limbo. The danger, it appears, starts when people retire, decide to take things easy and say they don't have to keep up with the world anymore. 'A vicious cycle sets in,' reported Schaie. 'If you don't do an activity any more, you begin losing the skills to do it. Then you are even less likely to engage in those activities.' The people who were almost too busy to be studied, Schaie said, were the ones who did very well.

Do You Lead With Your Eyes or Your Ears or...?

Think. How do you remember best?

Do you remember best when you see?

Do you remember best when you hear?

Do you remember best when you move some part of your body?

If you are eye-oriented, you'll remember best when you've used your eyes — reading a name, an address, a telephone number or other information. Leonardo da Vinci could paint a complete portrait after seeing his subject just once. Napoleon, with one glance at a military map, could remember every detail in it. If you are a musician, you'll visualise the written score as you play your instrument. If you often find yourself saying to somebody you're meeting for the second or third time, 'I'm sorry — I remember your face, but I can't recall your name,' it means you're eye-oriented. This is also the natural orientation that comes into play when you walk into a house for the first time and instantly feel you've been there before — the phenomenon we know as deja vu. It's usually interpreted as your having stayed in or visited that house in your previous birth. But what is more likely is that because you're eye-oriented, your memory has, on an earlier occasion, registered visiting a similar-looking place — and now your mind forms an immediate link between the house you're in and the one you'd visited earlier.

If you are ear-oriented, you retain more when you bring your sense of hearing into play. Hence, you'll pick up a foreign language through conversation, recognise voices immediately over the telephone, and be easily able to sing a song you hear just once. In a recently-reported case of assault-and-robbery, the Mumbai police were able to nab the culprit based only on a maidservant's assertion that he'd spoken in a familiar voice. Her attacker had worn a mask during the break-in, but in an identification line-up, Maria Minz was able (correctly, as it turned out from the later confession) to pick out the building's watchman as the culprit, based on only her recollection of the voice! Maria clearly was ear-oriented.

If you are movement-oriented, you'll master skills that involve movement of your limbs — like cycling, roller-skating, driving. Also you'll remember best when you use your hand to write a message, telephone number, or something else on paper. Even if you lose that piece of paper, you'll retain the written information without effort.

Do understand that this does not mean that you use only your eyes, ears or body movements as your aid to recall. Most often, we use a combination of these faculties. But to know which way you are naturally oriented helps you choose the study method that's best suited to you. Thus, if you are eye-oriented a correspondence course would suit you best. If you are ear-oriented, you'd learn best if you attended lectures. Or if your office hours and the lecture timings clash, you could still take up a correspondence course but read your study-material aloud to yourself. Similarly, if you are body-movement oriented you could write down notes whether you're reading or listening.

What is Your Orientation?

If you want to have some fun while finding out whether you are ear, eye or body movement-oriented, play this little word association game. You could try it out on your friends at a party and find out *their* orientation as well! Read each word and immediately write down the *first word* that springs to your mind. Spontaneity is essential: you should not be 'working out' your response.

Now, refer to the table, below, and see which word in each column most closely matches the one you've entered:

Game Word	Your Word
tea	
pen	
train	
clock	
fire	
playground	
Edison	
battle	
sing	
light	

Next, figure out which way you're oriented:

Column A contains words descriptive of visuals that are *seen* in connection with the game word.

Column B contains words that are connected to the game word by virtue of their *sound*.

Column C contains words that are associated with the game word in terms of *action*.

So, if your words most closely match those in:

Game Word	A	B	C
tea	cup	pea	drink
pen	nib	hen	write
train	track	brain	travel
clock	antique	ding-dong	wind
fire	flame	crackle	hire
playground	park	children	swing
Edison	bulb	scientist	electricity
battle	ground	guns	win
sing	song	music	playback
light	neon	bright	enlightenment

A: You are eye-oriented.

B: You are ear-oriented.

C: You are body movement-oriented.

An equal mix would mean that you tend to use all three orientations depending on the context or situation.

In conclusion:

Game Word : 'Clock'

'Antique'   'Ding-Dong'   'Wind'

- Limits on learning are self-imposed. Make the sky your limit by preparing fertile ground.
- Brain drain is *not* as inevitable as wrinkles and a slower 50-yard dash. Keep yourself intellectually challenged and you'll stay sharp well into your 80s.
- Exercise increases the flow of oxygen-rich blood to the brain,

promoting clear thinking and sharper recall.
- Optimism optimises recall.
- Know your natural orientation — and exploit it when you have a learning task on hand.
- Make concentration a habit — it should not be forced.
- Believe in yourself: you have more mental vigour than you think you do!

Workshop Extra

Play 'Buzzword Today'

The difference between a sharp memory and mushy thinking does not lie in good luck or good genes. Though some people appear to have been born with enviable memory power, the ability to learn and retain well is very largely a matter of the degree of stimulation you received in your childhood. If the stimulation was of a high degree, it stokes up a strong 'Learning Emotion' — a positive emotion that connects information to your feelings. When this connection clicks, you experience that intellectual high.

If your Learning Emotion is currently at a low ebb (or has never crested the big waves), how do you stimulate it now? I'm a strong believer in fun. Learning *must* be fun. So, I suggest you make a game of it. Play *Buzzword Today*.

It has got five simple steps:

1. Pick a new word.
2. Find out its correct pronounciation.
3. Find out its meaning.
4. Make it the buzzword of the day.
5. Now, practice.

Step 1. Pick a new word from the dictionary, one that you've never heard before. Say, you pick ARCHITRAVE.

Step 2. Figure out how you should pronounce it. The dictionary will tell you: ARK-I-TRAVE.

Step 3. Next, what is the meaning? 'Trim surrounding a doorway or window'. What's that? The explanation: 'A wooden panel that conceals the joint between a door frame and wall plaster.'

Step 4. Now, make this the buzzword of today!

Use it in any appropriate context during your conversation through the day:

- 'Should we have an *architrave* around our windows?'
  'No, the door slams due to the wind and the plaster loosens and falls. Let's put an *architrave* around the door.'
  'But will an *architrave* stop the plaster from loosening?'
  'Maybe ... maybe not. But the *architrave* will certainly conceal the cracks!'

or

- *While watching TV ...*
  'Look, the door that Anupam Kher just walked out of... It has an *architrave!*'

or

- *While eating dinner...*
  'I think this dish requires an *architrave*!'
  'Why should a dish need an *architrave*?'

'To conceal its taste! Isn't that what an architrave is meant to do? To conceal?' And so on.

Now if you were to just look up 'architrave' and its meaning in the dictionary (in the way you look up a number in the directory) and then get involved in your daily routine, you would remember it only for the time that it stayed in your short-term memory — perhaps only for the next hour or so. But, by playing *Buzzword Today*, you keep bringing up the word. And this repetition helps to push the word from your short-term memory into your long-term memory — and brand it there.

YUCK... BURNT AGAIN! I THINK I NEED AN ARCHITRAVE!

Learning and Memory. Mind games are a great way to learn! Buzzword today not only ensures that you learn a new word without great effort every day, but also that you remember it because it will have so many fun associations for you.

But, what does learning new words have to do with improving your memory? There's an improving link between the two. Language is the means by which you catalogue and store your memories. Take a simple word like 'elephant'. If there were no such word as 'elephant' in your vocabulary, there would be no visual or imprint of an 'elephant' in your mind. And when you hear the word 'elephant', it will bring forth no recollection or 'memory'.

There is another way that Buzzword Today boosts your memory. Its fun approach to learning enables your mind to transfer what is being learnt from short-term memory to long-term recall. We all have two types of memory:

Active and Super Active Memory. Short-term memory, or so called Active Memory, is a temporary storage facility. You use it when, for instance, you look up a number in the telephone directory and immediately dial it. When you've finished your conversation, you forget the number. You've used your short-term memory to aid you in carrying out a specific, short-term action.

In contrast to this, there is your long-term or Super Active Memory. This is the faculty that comes into play when you study for an exam, remember names and faces and anniversary dates — and also those telephone numbers that are so frequently dialled that you don't need to look them up in the directory.

As important as this repetition is *the way* you repeat the word. In the first place, doing it in a fun way, for instance as a joke at the dining table, makes retention easier. But even more, in *Buzzword* you're also repeating the word in its correct context — in relation to your windows and doors. This *meaning-in-context* helps to fix the word much more firmly in your mind.

Finally, you are not forcing yourself to mindlessly mutter 'architrave' all through the day like a mantra. You are giving yourself breaks in between, but returning to the word. These breaks are important because they give your sub-conscious time to chew on the new learning byte — and to absorb it.

Step 5. In and of itself, of course, *Buzzword Today* will not build the powerful memory you're seeking.

But practice in this game trains you in the four principles of Super Learning. To repeat, they are: *Fun* — for association; *Repetition* — for familiarity; *Meaning-in-context* — for fixing; and Breaks — for long-term retention.

So, this is how you should approach any information that you require to memorise:

First Principle of Super Learning: *I shall have fun.* Remember the Mary Poppins song, 'Just a spoonful of sugar helps the medicine go down'? That's the spirit in which you should approach any new learning task. It doesn't mean you should take the task so lightly that you don't really try. It means that you approach it earnestly but with a light heart. Don't get so serious that you put yourself under pressure to learn: that would make you unfocused. Forced concentration overstimulates the brain — which may explain why it's so easy to get derailed by an interruption when you're *trying* too hard, too seriously to concentrate.

I SHALL REPEAT...
I SHALL REPEAT...
I SHALL...

Second Principle of Super Learning: *I shall repeat.* 'Repeat' has two 're's built into it. Recitation and Review. You learn something. Then you move it from short-term to long-term memory by reciting it until it becomes familiar. As you go along, jot down questions relating to the study material on a piece of paper. When you feel you've memorised the material, look at your list of questions. Can you answer all of them? If you can't, go back to the text and read it over again, reciting those portions that relate to the questions you couldn't answer. This fills up the information gaps in your memory.

Third Principle of Super Learning: *I shall understand the meaning.* There are two kinds of 'meaning':

- The literal meaning: Take a short stanza from William Wordsworth's poem, *The Prelude*:

Fair seed-time had my soul, and I grew up
    Fostered alike by beauty and by fear:
Much favoured in my birthplace, and no less
    In that beloved Vale to which ere long
We were transplanted — there were we let loose
    For sports of wider range

You could learn this stanza by rote (by heart), without paying any attention to its meaning. But if you do grasp the meaning, you will naturally find it much easier to remember. Say aloud or write down the meaning of the poet's thought thus:
'My soul had enough (*fair*) time to grow (*seed-time*). I grew up, fostered by beauty and fear. Both, beauty and fear, were

much favoured in that beloved valley (*Vale*) to which we were transplanted before long (*ere long*). There in the vale we were let loose for sports of wider range.'

When you understand what the poet is trying to say, you are in effect *re-learning* his thoughts and making them your own. After this, it becomes easier to learn the poem because you *know* what he means and you are able to anticipate what's going to come.

• The meaning-in-context: Just as the meaning of a sentence puts it into an easy-to-understand framework, so does the meaning-in-context put it into an easy-to-link-and-remember framework.

For instance, if you try and learn by heart the dates below, you may or may not remember them accurately, or at the very least you'll have to put in a fair amount of effort to memorise them:

1946	The first session of the UN Assembly
1947	India and Pakistan become independent
1948	Mynmar (Burma) becomes independent
1949	General Mao Tse-Tung proclaims the People's Republic of China
1951	Libya becomes independent
1959	Chinese occupy Tibet
1964	Jawaharlal Nehru dies
1965	Sir Winston Churchill dies
1968	Martin Luther King assassinated
1969	US astronaut Neil Armstrong becomes the first man to set foot on the moon

Now, instead of trying to parrot these dates, try to first arrange them into a pattern to get the meaning-in-context:

Close on the heels of 1946, when the UN was first convened, several countries won their independence: 1947 — India and

Pakistan; next, in 1948 — Burma; 1949 — Mao's revolution; 1951 — Libya.

1959 was a bad year as Mao's China occupied Tibet, forcing the Dalai Lama to flee to India.

The 1960s saw great men dying, but also saw a giant leap being taken for mankind. In 1964, which is the reverse of 1946, the date we started out with (46 becomes 64), Nehru died, followed by Churchill in 1965 and King in 1968. At the fag-end of the 1960s, that is, in 1969, Neil Armstrong set foot upon the moon.

As you set down this string of events, each in the context of the others, you'll 'see' them arrange themselves into a logical pattern in your memory — and this will make it easier for you to summon them up in recall.

Fourth Principle of Super Learning: *I shall take breaks.* Learning breaks are not a waste of time, as they might seem, quite the opposite in fact. If you try to memorise continuously, it's like going into overdrive. You get all wound up with the effort and you have to keep trying harder to concentrate. At the end, you're not necessarily remembering anything better. The fact is, when you study, you're doing so with your conscious mind. If you go on gabbling non-stop, you're simply stuffing your conscious mind to take what you've learnt and to allow it to sink into your sub-conscious. Once it's absorbed at that deeper level, remembering it becomes an automatic reflex.

I was once asked whether sleeping after learning something aids or interferes with the learning process. There's no doubt that 'sleeping on it' helps! Perhaps for the same reason I've stated above: you switch your mind from overdrive to the relaxed mode. What's more, research has found that dreaming also helps learning. Sometimes the dreams that occur during sleep seem to be initially filled with fuzzy, insignificant details.

But then, suddenly things click. It's as if the trivia and clutter that were running interference with your memory have been got rid of, leaving only a clear picture and the important facts.

Recent studies at Israel's Weizmann Institute of Science suggest that dreaming helps to 'cement' memories of new information. The researchers reported that people who were awakened during the dream phase of sleep did not remember a learned task very well. But if allowed to sleep undisturbed, test subjects performed newly-learned tasks faster and better the next morning.

And One Last Thing...

Finally, don't forget that great motivator — the self-bribe. There's nothing like the lure of a reward at the end of an accomplishment to get you to work with a will at the most difficult lesson in the world — and to master it! It clears *all* mental blocks and gets the juices of that Learning Emotion flowing.

Admittedly, rewarding yourself is not really a memory strategy for the long term. You could end up doing something *only* to snatch that carrot at the end of the stick. And that's not the kind of mental conditioning I'd wish on anyone. So, use this incentive only to kickstart yourself, to get out of that initial inertia.

To re-cap, play *Buzzword Today* regularly so that you imbibe the principles of learning that it incorporates; then, apply these principles to other learning tasks. Let's tick them off:
- Make learning fun
- Repeat and review
- Try to understand the meaning and the meaning-in-context
- Take short breaks, even an occasional nap
- Get yourself off to a flying start by rewarding yourself — initially.

Chapter : 2

YES, YOU CAN...

Memorise a shopping list without using paper or pen

Remember a list of things-to-do in the right sequence

Even reel off a list of items backward if you want to!

TOOLS YOU'LL USE

Absurd 'action pictures'

The chain-association method

Visualisation exercises

AND YOU WILL...

Have a foolproof way of remembering everything you need to get done every day of your life!

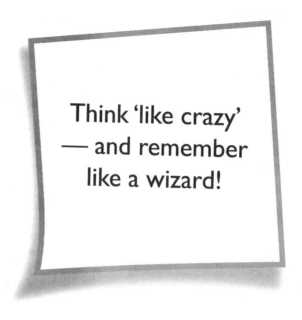

Think 'like crazy'
— and remember
like a wizard!

How to remember a list of errands
without making a list

Stalactites. Those are the icicle-like things that hang down from the roofs of caves, aren't they? Or, are those stalag*mites*? Never can remember? If ever there were a contest for confounding words, these two would be front-runners. Is there an easy way of remembering the difference? Enid Blyton, that well-loved creator of children's stories, devised a way.

Here's an extract from one of her Famous Five books (*Five go to Billycock Hill*) that reveals the memory trick she used:

'This sounds good,' said Julian. 'Let's see — what did Toby tell us about the caves?'

'They're thousands of years old — they've got stalagmites and stalactites,' said George. 'Oh, I know what those are,' said Anne. 'They look like icicles hanging from the roof — while below, on the floor of the cave, other icicles seem to grow upwards to meet them!'

'Yes — the roof ones are stalac*tites* and the ground ones are stalag*mites*,' said Dick. 'I simply never can remember which is which,' said Anne.

'It's easy!' said Julian. 'The stalactite icicles have to hold *tight* to the roof — and the stalag*mite* ones *might* some day join with the ones above them!' The others laughed. 'I shall never forget which are which now,' said Anne.

Nor will most children — or adults — who read that bit. What did Enid Blyton do to make the difference between stalagmites and stalactites unforgettable? She used one of the most powerful memory tricks known — creating mind-pictures that make the words they relate to unforgettable. You picture those icicles holding *tight* to the roof, and you'll never forget they are stalac*tites*. And likewise, the ones growing upwards from the ground, and which *might* someday meet the ones hanging down from the roof — those, of course, are the stalag*mites*!

Too often we try to memorise things abstractly, ignoring the physical reality of a bit of data. But if you make a habit of associating the word or information you wish to recall with something concrete, you'll make retention that much easier. And if the association is a humorous or a cute one, the memory will be even stronger because the emotions are involved.

Mind Pictures: Why we Remember Nicknames Better

This is probably the reason we remember nicknames much better than real names. Long years into adulthood, you may well have forgotten the names of your high-school teachers, but you'll never forget the name which you and your school chums called your Math master out of his hearing — 'Four

Eyes', because he wore spectacles; or, your English mistress — 'Moon Face', because she hadn't yet seemed to have got rid of her baby fat. Because those visual images are indelibly etched into your mind, the nicknames are, too. I've witnessed several incidents where an adult meets, say, a 25-year-old after an interval of two decades. She has last seen this young woman as a cherubic five-year-old, and her greeting now is something on the lines of a delighted, 'Sparrow! How you've grown! Remember I used to call you Sparrow because you held your lips like a beak when you were hungry? Like a baby sparrow ...!'

Again, as we see, the adult remembers not the real name of the child she had last met many moons ago ... but the affectionate nickname she had bestowed on this child. And her delighted exclamation shows she can still picture the 'little sparrow' with whom she had associated the little girl!

Memorable Associations. *That* is what mnemonics (or memory-improving techniques) are all about. And all of us make such associations all the time. For instance, many of us associate bread with butter, or cup with saucer, these are associations based on daily habits — unlike the 'Little Sparrow' association, which has the adult remembering the affectionate sobriquet she had endowed on a five-year-old 20 years ago. Extend the affectionate to the absurd, the crazy ... and you get associations that are even more unforgettable! So, in mnemonics, if you were to associate, say, tea and toast, you'd have the toast jumping up and down in the tea, or hovering above it like a levitating *sadhu*, or perhaps turning somersaults in it!

These, of course, are not the kinds of things that happen while you're sedately sipping your tea or dipping your toast into it, but the very absurdity of the images, their comical aspect itself, creates such memorable mind-pictures that you cannot but remember the association ... tea-and-toast. Try it now ... 'see' in your mind's eye that toast

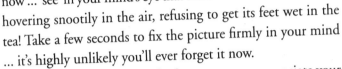

hovering snootily in the air, refusing to get its feet wet in the tea! Take a few seconds to fix the picture firmly in your mind ... it's highly unlikely you'll ever forget it now.

Let's take another example. Say, you want to associate your wall-clock with the tubelight in your bedroom. So, here are the two words you need to associate: 'wall-clock' and 'tubelight'. Well, now imagine that wall-clock scowling at a grinning tubelight, the scowl growing ever more fierce the more the tubelight does its Cheshire-cat routine. Or, imagine the wall-clock biffing the tubelight with its two hands! Or the wall-clock plucking the tubelight off its fixings and using it as a straw to drink its cola! I'm sure you're smiling already at those crazy images. Good! That means you are 'seeing' them in your mind. From here, it's a short step to creating your own comical, silly, absurd images.

If you initially find yourself wondering whether you can be so 'imaginative', don't let it worry you. Your mind is a great interpreter. Stimulated, it can make you a first-rate visual artist. In the Workshop that follows this chapter, you'll find ways in which you can provide it with just this kind of stimulation.

Keep two important things in mind when you begin the

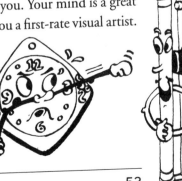

creative exercise of associating words with images:

First, work with only two items at a time. If there are 10 items, first take item 1 and 2, then item 2 and 3, then 3 and 4 ... and so on. This way, you progress in a simple one-to-the-next chain that does not strain your mind.

Second, visualise from left to right. So, you'll have your wall-clock on the left, biffing the tubelight on the right, for instance. This helps you to keep the chain in its proper sequence. Besides, that's how you read most languages — from left to right.

Let me demonstrate these two guidelines.

Read the list of 6 items below and follow how we're going to create our 'absurd associations':

1. pen
2. cat
3. bottle
4. spectacles
5. bus
6. helicopter

You are going to memorise this list by summoning up some unforgettable mind-pictures.

First, we'll see the pen writing on the cat's back. Or better yet, 'see' several pens writing on several cats' backs. Hold that picture in your mind for some time. Concentrate on it. Fix it firmly in your imagination. Once you've done that, move on ...

Now, conjure up the next picture. The cat is chasing the bottle. A crazy, comical animation that re-enacts the cartoons you see on screen. Just picture that feline, deadly intent on her game, her tail rigidly up, running in hot pursuit of the bottle! And picture that poor nervous bottle, stumbling awkwardly ahead, barely able to keep out of reach of that ferocious cat! This is one chase you're not likely to forget in a hurry! On to the next visual now ...

Now you see the bottle sloshing out several tiny spectacles from its mouth. Just look at that bottle spewing out thousands upon thousands of minuscule spectacles from its mouth. Can you just see that deluge of spectacles tumbling out of that bottle? You can ... and once you've burned that visual into an indelible mind picture, you can move on.

The spectacles now leap straight on to its headlights, off again. See that mischievous glint in as they jump on and off the bus. On and off, on and off. No wonder that bus is looking so bewildered as its headlights dim and brighten, dim and brighten, dancing to the tune of those bullying, bouncing spectacles! Unforgettable!

Next, the bus is picked up by the helicopter. And together, they fly in the sky! The bus doesn't know what's 'got' it. And the helicopter is grinning as it dangles the bus in its 'claws'! Ever imagined a helicopter ferrying a bus across the clear blue sky? Imagine it now!

There ... that was a painless exercise, wasn't it? And see how easily you remember the list of items in the right order because of the absurd associations you've created and the strong action pictures you've used:

The **pen** scribbling on the **cat** ...

The **cat** chasing the **bottle** ...

The **bottle** spouting **spectacles** ...

The **spectacles** jumping on and off the **bus** ...

The **bus** flying with the helicopter ...

The **helicopter** ...

Now, stop right there to catch your breath, mentally speaking ... and to pat yourself on the back, because you've done it! You've taken a list of items. Linked the first to the second, the second to the third, in a chain of crazy mind pictures. And, by remembering those tag-teamed associations, you've also memorised the list of items in their correct order.

Have you noticed one more important thing that has emerged in this absurd-association method? It's the power of action-words. Or the power of the verb. The pen **writes** ... the cat **chases** ... the bottle **spouts** ... the spectacles **jump** ... the bus **flies** ... the helicopter **picks up**. The use of these different verbs has helped to create those action pictures in your mind — and 'action shots' are what have made the images so memorable.

So let's review the process, step by step. What have we learned about the art and practice of absurd association?

- You pick two items, for example, 'pen' and 'cat'.
- You think of an action, a verb to associate them.
- You picture the pen and the cat in this action.

The left-to-right visualisation is really important only for the beginner. Once you grasp the technique and get some practice in using it, you needn't flog the left-to-right dictum too much.

This is the way it goes:

Items ⇨ Action ⇨ Image = Association

Also, with practice, you'll be able to reel off the list backwards: helicopter ... bus ... spectacles ... bottle ... cat ... pen.

Practice is the key. So, get going. Make your own lists. Start with six items. As you become more adept, you'll be able to add on more items. Don't let bashfulness hold you back from allowing your imagination free rein to create whatever absurd associations it will. The ones you create will be far more memorable (for you) than the ones that I or anyone else might create for you.

All it takes really is practice. So practise when you're on your own. Practise with your family. Practise with your friends. Make it into a game at your parties, or a lunch-hour contest with your colleagues. Practise ... practise ... practise.

Once you develop this knack of creating absurd associations, you'll be able to move on to the next stage: applying this technique to remembering items on a shopping list or a list of things-to-do.

How to Remember a List of 'Things-I-must-do-today'

You might want to ask, 'What's wrong with just writing down a list of the things I must get done and then referring to this list as I go through the day?' I'm not against writing down a list, whether it's a shopping list or a blow-by-blow itemisation of chores that need to be completed on a particular day. But I know several people who genuinely forget to refer to that list, and others who simply neglect to carry it along with them. There are other risks: the memory pad can be misplaced, or the piece of paper can fly off your table and out of the window!

Sometimes, of course, forgetfulness is not the only problem, or even the chief one. Some people *remember* all the things they need to buy, or all the errands they need to run. But, because

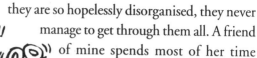

they are so hopelessly disorganised, they never manage to get through them all. A friend of mine spends most of her time travelling to and fro several times. She remembers each of the various tasks she has to tackle, but manages to accomplish only a few because she refuses to organise herself.

An ordered mind is an important companion to memory. I'm constantly fascinated by the organisational skills displayed by the chefs in the original Indian fast-food restaurants — our South Indian *Udipi* restaurants! The chef gets several orders tumbling in one upon the other, and he manages them all simultaneously and efficiently. He spreads the *dosa* mixture on the heated pan, pours the *idli* batter into the sieved vessels and puts them to steam, stirs the *bhaji* filling for the *dosa*, puts on the filter coffee to brew. His ingredients have been placed close at hand for easy reaching-out. His fine-tuning is so perfect that he never burns a dosa. Yet, every order is quickly dispensed to the counter in a few minutes, to be picked up by the waiter and served, fresh and hot, to the customer.

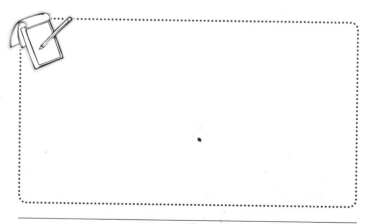

We can borrow a leaf from this chef's book to organise our shopping and other errands for the day in the shortest possible time. After all, who wants to be stressed out simply because she or he forgot, or didn't get around to, say, picking up a ballpoint refill? So, let's get cracking on that to-do list.

First, we'll figure out the various chores that need to be done. An illustrative list might read:

1. Buy vegetables.
2. Take music system to be repaired.
3. Attend PTA meeting.
4. Buy birthday gift for friend.
5. Visit friend at home.
6. Buy postage stamps.
7. Fill petrol in car.
8. Sign up for aerobic dance lessons and pay advance fee.
    Phew! You've got a busy day ahead of you!

Prepare: In one place, pile up all the different things you're going to need to accomplish your various chores. They will also serve as your memory cues: shopping basket for vegetables; music system; notes, if any, for PTA meeting; sufficient cash or your credit card in your wallet.

Plan Ahead: This is mostly common sense. Except for the PTA meeting which will be at a fixed time, the rest of the errands can be done at any time — except that you need to remember that the local post office downs its stationery shutters at 3 p.m. So, organise your various chores around the PTA meeting and the visit to the post-office. Anticipate and factor in some time that might be spent waiting at the petrol station if there's a queue; that gives you a cushioning time block.

Next, plan your route so that you don't waste time driving

to and fro. And, once again, common sense will tell you that vegetables, being perishable items, should be purchased last if possible, keeping the other considerations in mind.

At the end of this careful planning exercise, your final list might look something like this:

1. Fill **petrol** in car.
2. Take **music system** for repairs.
3. Sign up for aerobic dance lessons and pay advance **fee**.
4. Buy **postal stamps**.
5. Attend **Parent-Teacher Association** meeting.
6. Buy **birthday gift** for friend.
7. Visit **friend**.
8. Buy **vegetables** on the way back home.

You may feel that all this elaborate planning and preparing is far too fussy an exercise to engage in every morning. But you'd be surprised at how quickly a disorganised person forgets what he or she has to do! For instance, at the PTA meeting you could get so involved that, still thinking about what was under discussion, you might drive off straightaway to your friend's place. And, ringing the doorbell, you'd possibly remember that you'd forgotten to pick up a gift! Everyday situations are full of red herrings. But you can sidestep them by, first, planning ahead, and then using the chain-association method to arm yourself with a foolproof way of remembering everything you need to get done.

So let's move on now to conjuring up some unforgettable mind-pictures in a chain that links the chores on our ordered list. Look at the list again and note the words in bold type:

| petrol | music system | fee | postal stamps |
| teacher | birthday gift | friend | vegetables |

What we have done is to select one tangible word from each errand. Now let's start the chain-association process, creating pictures that are as memorably absurd as possible. Take two items at a time.

1. The petrol hose drowns your music system by cascading petrol over it. Picture that: a frisky hose merrily letting loose on your hapless music system which is struggling to surface above the engulfing pool of petrol.

   Got your mental grapplers on that image? Move on.

2. The music system belches out the fee money instead of music. Currency notes fly out of it and into the air. More and more of them. Visualise it strongly. Move on.

3. The fee money dances with the tiny postal stamps. Oh, they're having a jolly session as their little toes twinkle in time to a lively tune. Paint this comical picture on your mental monitor. When you can see it clearly, go to the next ...

4. The postal stamp is standing with chalk before a blackboard and is teaching calculations to the senior Math teacher in your son's school. She is seated, prim, stern and bespectacled, at a desk, while the postal stamp holds forth. Imagine that cheeky, two-rupee stamp teaching the teacher! Ridiculous? Then that's exactly why you'll never forget the picture. The more absurd, the better as far as remembering is concerned!

5. The teacher is struggling desperately to open a giant-sized birthday gift. She looks like an ant in relation to that huge, wrapped and beribboned package. You've seen enough films in the Honey-I've-shrunk-the-kids genre to summon up a hilarious I've-shrunk-the-teacher visual. You won't forget this one. Go on.

6. The gift jumps on to a see-saw, with your friend sitting on the opposite end. And each time it jumps, the see-saw goes up and down. You'll chortle at this picture, and later on, you'll tell your friend about it and the both of you will laugh together again. On to ...

7. Your friend opens the refrigerator and reels back, stunned, as a swarming horde of vegetables jumps out of it. See them leap through the air — especially your favourite aubergines, bright and plump in their jaunty purple robes! The onslaught seems without end. And your friend is rooted to the spot, dumbstruck and bewildered. Can't you just see that crazy scene!

Now review all those images in order: the petrol hose submerging your music system ... your tape recorder 'belting out' the fee money ... the fee money dancing with the postal stamps ... the postal stamp teaching the teacher ... the teacher struggling to open the giant-sized gift ... the gift see-sawing with your friend ... your friend staring horror-struck at the vegetables jumping out of the fridge! You can be sure that, because of the exaggerated absurdity of these images, you won't forget a single errand you need to run that day, a single item you need to buy!

Though, initially, you may think it's far easier to simply carry a list and refer to it instead of going through this entire association process, such thinking is only a mirage. If you haven't been used to allowing your imagination free rein (as, for instance, in regular day-dreaming), you may need to nudge along the process in the initial stages. But, as you practise, you'll find yourself breezing through your inner-animated cartoons with the ease of a veteran.

You'll be having fun even as you strengthen your memory force. And you'll reap side-benefits, too:

- You'll have a laugh a day and be in a better mood for it.
- You'll find the mind-pictures you create funny enough to narrate to your friends and spread some more laughter around. You may even start a trend.
- As you train and exercise your imagination in the absurd-association method, you'll find yourself becoming more mentally creative in other areas of your life, too, whether it's creating graphics for an ad campaign or devising a new game for your five-year-old's birthday party.
- You'll also develop a humorous perspective on situations which will help you take life's googlies in your stride.

And to think you hadn't expected any of these benefits when you set off on your journey to sharpen your memory skills!

Workshop Extra

Your Personal Guide to Absurd Association

How did you react to the preceding chapter? I hope it tickled your sense of humour as much as it stirred up your imagination! If you're still hesitating because of doubts and questions that might be nagging at your mind, this Workshop is specially aimed at clearing those doubts and giving you tips and pointers on how you can take the art of absurd association to a personal high.

Thinking in Mind-Pictures Comes Naturally to Us All

During the first eight months of your life, before you got around to doing things with your hands and legs, it was your eyes that were your beacon to the new world around. During your waking hours, they were constantly on the move, darting around and taking in all the sights that came within their ken. And this, probably, is the reason that your sense of sight is the most developed of all the six senses, the reason it can imprint images and impressions so vividly and so memorably in your mind.

This is the principle that mnemonics has latched on to: the fact that thinking in *pictures* can create indelible imprints in the mind, and that this ability can help us remember better than just relying on parrot-like repetition or trying to remember words or numbers off a page. Transform anything you want to remember into an interesting visual and you've taken the most important step towards remembering it.

You Can Do It Easily — and Here's the Proof!

You don't really need me to tell you how to dream up interesting visuals. You do it all the time! However, if you need confirmation of your natural ability, try this simple visualisation exercise:

Relax and let your mind gradually sieve out current preoccupations and concerns. Now, take yourself back in time to a day in your childhood. See yourself once again in your parents' home. See what you're wearing — your favourite childhood dungarees and T-shirt, perhaps. It's a school holiday and you're running towards the front door because the outdoors is beckoning so invitingly. You open the door and see, yes, it's a lovely, sunshiny day, and there's even a cool breeze blowing. You take in deep, full breaths of that fresh, clean air, you listen to the sparrows chittering in the trees that border your house, you look up at the cloudless blue sky, and you feel that *joie de vivre* racing through your veins. The happy world of the morning beckons — and you see yourself leaping down the steps to meet it ...

Even as you read these words, you'll find you are already seeing and feeling what it was to be a child in those bygone days.

Similarly, try visualising other situations: the most enjoyable party you ever went to, watching a telecast of your favourite sport with your favourite team winning, a dream date. You will know you are visualising effectively when you feel those subtle sensations — a pickling of your scalp, a tingling down your spine.

So you see, you can do it — you are already doing it!

And, Very Soon, You'll be Doing it With Speed

You might be bothered by the feeling that you'll never be able to create mind-pictures fast enough to use the association method effectively. Rest assured that, sooner than you know it, you'll be spinning out those graphics as fast as you need to. Remember when you first began to learn driving? Initially you felt that you'd never be able to coordinate all those various reflexes even as you watched the road — keep your foot on the clutch and accelerator or clutch and brake, hands on the wheel but also at the ready to change gears. But soon enough you were driving that car, each reflex switching on smoothly when required. Similarly, with some practice, you'll find your mental gears switching on pictures and creating absurd associations as and when you need them.

Exaggeration is the Key

The more imaginative and exaggerated your pictorial associations, the better you'll remember them. And exaggeration is an art that comes naturally to us when the need arises. Which of us hasn't exaggerated a situation at some time or the other? A little lacing and trimming while narrating an anecdote to an interested audience, a bit of overemphasising — or a full-blown fiction — of how one stood up to the class bully or the boss! An inclination to showmanship is naturally inherent in each of us. And it's this natural gift that you must exploit to the fullest in creating your absurd associations. Exaggeration makes them unusual, freakish, unique! And because they are all your own, you'll recall them with hardly any effort.

Motion Makes It Even More Memorable

Anything that moves catches your eye more effectively than a still-life does. You may stop to look at the display of merchandise in a shop window, but if a clever shop-keeper has outfitted his showcase with a mannequin that pirouettes, it will *definitely* catch your attention. Similarly, if a friend sees you across the street, he'll wave his hand so that the movement catches your eye. For the same reason, you're likely to remember images from a motion picture for a longer time than a display of slides.

The fact that motion makes pictures memorable is the reason we put 'action verbs' into our absurd-association pictures. I do realise that, in the beginning particularly, you may not be able to summon up action words in the blink of an eye! So, to give you that initial momentum, I'm providing you with a list of action verbs below. Refer to them now and then if you need to. Eventually, as you get action-verb-oriented, you won't need a reference list of verbs.

I'll just emphasise one more tip: drama is essential. Your association will be more vivid if, for example, the pen *serenaded* the cat rather than just sang to it. But I leave it to you to make your personal contribution to these association dramatics!

Your Action-Verb List:

slamming	see-sawing
somersaulting	toppling
cutting	smashing
crushing	tearing
chomping	catapulting
kicking	intertwining
breaking	punching
biting	jumping
licking	drowning
nudging	running

But, Will You Remember the Right Word?

You might still be troubled by this doubt: what if, after all your absurd-association exercises, you don't remember the right word? To illustrate this possibility, let me reproduce a joke I read in the 'Laughter, the Best Medicine' column of the *Reader's Digest*, by Liau Eng Siong of Malaysia:

John was visiting Japan for the first time. Everything about the country fascinated him: the people, the culture, and especially the language. A friend took him to dine at a restaurant. 'How do you say "Thank you" in Japanese?' John asked.

'Thank you is "ARI-GA-TO",' his friend answered. 'To help you remember, just think of "ALLIGATOR." It sounds like "ARIGATO."'

John practised saying it and seemed quite comfortable with the new word. At the end of the meal, John wanted to express his appreciation to the waiter, but could not remember how to say it. To remind him, his friend used his arms to imitate the reptile opening and closing its jaws.

'Ah!' John remembered He turned to the waiter and said loudly, 'CROCODILE! CROCODILE!'

Yes, I agree this kind of thing can happen. And it happened because the attempt here was merely to find a familiar word that sounded similar to the one that had to be remembered. There was no action verb to firmly associate 'Arigato' with 'alligator'. But suppose John had imagined that an alligator had got his jaws into his arm and he, unfazed by the alligator's unwanted attentions, was chanting, 'Later, later, alligator!'. The action, and the absurdity of his telling the alligator to eat him later would have fixed the association firmly in his mind — you can be sure he would have remembered it!

And no, he wouldn't have told the waiter, ALLIGATOR, instead of ARIGATO! When you're using this method, you *know* that you're making associations in order to remember things. If you practise with concentration, you'll find, eventually, that the associations fade, but you still remember the word you originally wanted to. It's little like a hologram where, when you view it from a certain distance or angle, the whole picture suddenly clicks into focus.

List One	List Two	List Three
boot	ruler	book
bucket	globe	Mars
train	flower	television
trousers	coaster	shirt
ball	aeroplane	ashtray
gas-stove	wrist-watch	lamp
	telephone	table
	chandelier	earring
		bicycle
		camel

And One Last Thing: Practise, Practise ... Just Do It!

Practice is critical to making this association method a matter of habit, almost second nature when you are faced with a remembering task. You have already started with the list I provided in the chapter that precedes this Workshop. Now, challenge yourself some more. Memorise the lists below, using action verbs to associate one item with the next in the chain-association method. Start with the short list, the first one. Then go on to the longer lists:

Let's review how you'll go about it:

1. Take up the first two items to be associated. For instance: 'boot' and 'bucket' from the first list.

2. Associate them with an outlandish kind of action — the boot thwacking the bucket, for example.

3. Fix the visual firmly in your mind.

4. Move on to the next two items in the chain — bucket and train.

Once you've practised with these lists, make up your own and practise with those. Then ask your friends to make up more lists and visualise your way through those. Enjoy the entire process; don't look on mistakes as setbacks, just have a good laugh and continue. I envy you your first round of applause from an admiring audience!

Chapter **3**

YES, YOU CAN...

Remember the names of several strangers you've met in a single evening

Remember any name (or names) ... for a lifetime if need be

Sow seeds of friendship, goodwill and warmth

TOOLS YOU'LL USE

Social Graces

The Power of Personal Association

Silly Substitution

The Sounds of Music

The Signs of the Zodiac

AND YOU WILL...

Never again have to say, 'I'm sorry, but I have a poor memory for names...'

How to remember names

12 easy ways to boost recall!

What's your most dreaded nightmare on a social occasion? For many people, it's a somewhat familiar face bouncing into their line of vision with a loudly querying, 'Don't you remember me?' You don't. And what you've particularly forgotten is his name (or hers). What do you do in the face of that sometimes-impossible-to-answer question without giving offence? Quick witted men have fielded that googly in clever ways. Whenever a man asked Charles Michelson, the late publicity director for the Democratic National Committee, 'Do you remember me?' — and he didn't — he said, 'yes — and it turned out you were right, didn't it?'

But in the scramble to get out of a tight spot with the help of a quick wit, social graces can sometimes be the first casualty. Charles Bay, former U.S. Ambassador to Norway, once answered that tricky query with, 'Sure, I remember you. Say, how'd you ever get out of that trouble you were in?' Winston Churchill was even more willing to squelch the unfortunate poser of the question, 'Do you remember me?' with the reply, 'Why should I?'

Most of us would balk at wit that borders on discourtesy. And in social interactions, politeness supersedes wit as an asset. In this specific area of remembering the name of a person you've obviously met and been introduced to before, you know for sure that he's going to feel deflated if you don't remember his name; after all, you'd feel insulted in his place. And, on the other hand, you also know how great it feels when someone remembers your name after an interval. It vindicates your personhood and you feel flattered. And since this sets up such positive vibes between you and the other person, you're more warmly disposed to him, more likely to lend a ear, even a helping hand should he need it.

Whats in a Name? A Great Deal!

That's how much there is in remembering a name. But I want us to go beyond ulterior motives. A name is a symbol of our self. Remembering someone's name is recognising that self as special. It sows a seed of friendship. Generates warmth and understanding between two people and goodwill and harmony. When you say, 'Hello, Joshua!' the second time you meet him, the unspoken message you're also sending is, 'Hello, Joshua, I happy to know you.' It's the latter, unstated

HELLO GURUPADAPPAH!

WOW SHE REMEMBERS ME!

part of your greeting — 'I am happy to know you' — that makes Joshua smile warmly at you. You *remembered* his name … you reinforced his sense of self … and you've added to the sum of happiness in the little orbit that encloses the two of you.

We already know this. Which is why, though some people apologetically say to someone they're meeting for the second time, 'I'm sorry, I have a poor memory for names', I prefer the approach that some others adopt, which is to try and find out the name by asking a mutual acquaintance. I'll explain why.

If you always say, 'I have a poor memory for names,' you reinforce that conviction in your own mind and, in effect, *make* this negative attribute a part of your personality. Why persuade yourself about something that's not only negative but also untrue? Why not, instead, tell yourself, 'I *can* remember names, I *shall* remember names,' — since that, in any case, is true?

Two Kinds of Poor 'People Memory'

There's a vital difference between remembering things and remembering people: you don't bump into things, you *do* bump into people unexpectedly — at a crossing, a function, a shop, a party, a sale, *anywhere*! This means that you should be able to recognise a face as well as remember the name that goes with it when you're not prepared for it. So, while the absurd-association method can also be applied to people, you need in addition that something extra so that you are not caught unawares, with mind blank, when the Big Bump occurs!

There are two kinds of Poor People Memory:

1. **Poor Name Memory** : You don't recall ever meeting the person — which means you have a poor memory for faces.
2. **Poor Face Memory** : You recall having met the person, but can't, for the life of you, recall his name — which means you have a poor memory for names.

If you can't recall the face at all, chances are you'll be completely blank about the name. This is because normally our **visual sense is stronger on recall** than our sense of hearing. This is why I devote a separate chapter to remembering faces. The present chapter deals with the more common experience expressed in the apologetic, 'I remember your face, but I'm sorry I can't remember your name.'

There are two steps here:

1. To file away the name in your short-term memory, and then
2. To file away the name in your long-term memory.

Reinforcing Active Memory: Filing the Name for the Short Term

This serves the immediate purpose of politeness. And you can hone your short-term memory by using the strategy of simple social graces:

Be Sincerely Interested in the Other Person. This is of course the first social grace to be acquired. Being absent-minded or aloof at a party or other social event is nothing short of bad manners. If you aren't interested in the person you are being introduced to, you are hardly likely to remember the name. And if it's a long, slightly tough-on-the-tongue name, your attitude is likely to be, 'I'll never remember that name, and I couldn't care anyway.' You'll probably have forgotten it the next instant.

Interest, as I said in an earlier chapter, is critical to remembering. If you're not interested, your mind won't absorb, and without absorption there is no retention.

Make Sure You Hear the Name Clearly. Often, it's not that you forget the name soon after you've been introduced to someone, but that *you do not hear* it due to a mumbled introduction or one made in an accent that's alien to your ears. Also, sometimes the person making the introductions *knows* your name, but does not remember the name of the person s/he wants to introduce to you. So, if your name is, say, Sandeep, the introducer introduces *only* you with a bright, 'Meet my friend, Sandeep!' I've also encountered a typically Indian practice where a male acquaintance with his wife in tow, walks across the room towards me and says, 'This is my wife.' For some unfathomable reason, many Indian men never mention their wife's name while introducing her!

Let's see how you can tackle these situations. If your friend introduces only you, saying, 'Meet my friend, Sandeep,' never ask him to repeat the stranger's name to you. Obviously he doesn't remember, and your query would only embarrass him. First, greet the stranger with a normal, courteous, 'Pleased to meet you.' Then, immediately inquire, 'Sorry, I didn't quite catch your name.' There's no need to be embarrassed. Be direct and ask the name right out. People feel flattered if you make the effort. And when the person replies, for instance, 'Shivika,' repeat it thoughtfully, 'Ah, Shivika.' Then request her, 'Do you mind spelling it out, please?' She will be happy to oblige, 'S-H-I-V-I-K-A ... Shivika.'

This takes care of the clarity. For example, you'll know for sure that the middle consonant is 'v' and not 'b'. This is important: I know a Kovoor who is constantly being referred to as Kapoor. And I can tell you it doesn't please him one bit!

If it happens to be an uncommon name that you have never heard before, say so *and* take the opportunity to repeat the name: 'What an unusual name — Shivika'. To reinforce your short-term memory, you could then ask, 'What does it mean?'

Of course, not everybody knows what their name stands for, but if the person does, it's a further boost to remembering it. In this particular case, the woman may tell you, 'It means, "little Shiv." The suffix, *ika*, means "small" or "little", so — Shivika: little Shiv.' Now, that makes it so much easier to remember her name. Shiv is a deity's name, so that stranger is a little deity, a little Shiv — Shivika! And don't hold yourself back from going into this kind of detail about the meaning of a name because you think it will take up too much time. It's an effective ice-breaker — and nobody minds a little time spent on their name: on the contrary, they'll be flattered by your interest!

If the person is unaware of the meaning of her/his name, or even if you do get the meaning and carefully fix it in your memory, you can go one step further in reinforcing your short-term recall of it: in the course of the ensuing conversation, use the name as often as you can without, of course, going overboard. Say, 'What do you think, Shivika?' Or, 'What are your interests, Shivika?' Until, finally, 'Good night, Shivika!'

On the other hand, if the name is a familiar one to you, say so immediately: 'What a coincidence! My best friend is also called Shivika!' This association with your best friend's name (or with the name of a relative or close colleague) helps to further impress the name in your memory, so make a point of saying it out loud.

Now let's come to the man who doesn't care to introduce his wife by name! Let's call him 'Mukesh Sharma'. Of course, if all of you are on extremely formal terms, you'll probably just greet her with a 'Pleased to meet you, Mrs Sharma' — her married surname. In the case of a more informal setting, you can use the same memory-enhancing methods we applied in the case of 'Shivika':

- Take an interest in her as a person. Don't be influenced by the attitude of the husband who doesn't seem to attach much importance to her personhood. She has a name and identity beyond 'Mrs Sharma'.

- Ask her for her name directly. Say, her name is 'Mukta'. Make sure you hear it clearly.
- You repeat her name. Unless it is an all too familiar one, ask her to spell it out.
- You repeat the spelling. And say her name once again after you have spelled it out.
- If it's an uncommon name, you enquire about the meaning.
- If it's familiar name to you because a friend or other person known to you also bears it, you say so.
- During the conversation, suffix — or prefix — the name to your sentences as often as possible, ending with, 'Goodnight, Mukta'.

Often, just employing these social graces is enough to enable you to remember the name at that particular meeting or occasion, and even over the next few days. However, to fix it in your memory for the long term, there are other, more effective methods you can use — techniques that will help you remember for a lifetime if need be!

Reinforcing Super Active Memory: Filing the Name in Your Long-term Memory

There are various approaches that have been found to enhance name-remembering over the long haul. We'll start with the first and the best of them all:

Invest a Personal Meaning in the Name. A me-to-you connection can often cement the name forever in your mind. For instance, a friend of mine met a Dutch gentleman whose name was Hofstede. It was by no means a familiar name to her. But, in the course of the conversation they discovered that they shared a common birth-date: August, the ninth. The coincidence impacted so strongly on her mind that she remembered his name ever after — though they never met again. Such is the power of personal association!

You might wonder why she should remember the name, Hofstede, and not just the common birth-date? The reason is that when something unusual, or amazingly coincidental, hits you, it not only makes an impact on you mentally but also stirs up your emotions, and the combined effect results in a lasting impression. In this case, my friend immediately saw in Hofstede leonine qualities (birth sign: Leo) of leadership, self-assurance, etcetera that she felt were attributes she herself possessed. So intensely did she identify with him that his name itself became an indelible part of her memory bank.

Investing a personal meaning in a name makes remembering it effortless — *because the reference already exists in your memory.* The reference could be the name of a celebrity, a music group, a film, a river, mountain, city, saint, God ... Make the connection and you will remember the name for all your life. The reference name need not always be identical to the name you want to remember — a close similarity will suffice. Some examples are given in table (top) on page 80.

To get you on track with *similar references* you can associate with newly-introduced names of people, here are a few given in table (bottom) on page 80.

Obviously, not every name will have a famous reference that you can peg it to. But these are excellent mind-setters when you can! Use ingenuity to invest *personal* meaning into your chosen association. Thus, if you're a sports fan, you will probably find it most memorable to associate the name with a sports personality. A movie buff will tag it to a film celebrity. And so forth.

Name introduced	Associated with	Famous Name
Indian Ocean	music group	Indian Ocean
Usha	singer	Usha Iyer
Taylor	actress	Liz Taylor
Mohandas	social reformer; India's 'Father of the Nation'	Mohandas K. Gandhi
Robin	actor	Robin Williams
Anastasia	film	Anastasia
Sunil	cricketer	Sunil Gavaskar
Whitney	singer	Whitney Houston
Mohammed	prophet	Mohammed
Jhelum	river	Jhelum
Himalaya	mountain range	Himalayas
Vishnu	Indian God	Vishnu
Bellona	Roman goddess of war	Bellona
Jamshed	city	Jamshedpur

Name introduced	Associated with	Famous Name
Jawahar	Indian Prime Minister	Jawaharlal Nehru
Abram	American President	Abraham Lincoln
Saroj	poetess	Sarojini Naidu
Simran	Pakistani cricketer	Imran Khan
Kanchan	mountain range	Kanchenjunga
Behari	state in India	Bihar
Amit	actor	Amitabh Bachchan
Armaity	god	Almighty
Indu	Indian Prime Minister	Indira Gandhi

Now let's move on to names that might have no famous name you can hitch them to. Here, I'd recommend one of three options:

Use Absurd Association

We've already seen how knowing the meaning of a name can help to fix it in your short-term memory. Remember 'Shivika' or 'little Shiv'? Sometimes, however, the meaning may be so commonplace that merely knowing the meaning will not be enough to anchor it in your long-term memory. Take, for instance, a name like Kamal. You know that Kamal means lotus. But simply trying to remember his name by remembering its meaning may not work for you — or for most people. It's just too commonplace to be memorable. So how do you go about making this commonplace meaning more memorable? Yes, of course you remember — by making the commonplace uncommon, absurd! Which takes us right back to our absurd-association method.

So, if you're introduced to someone called Kamal, create a quick and arresting picture of him standing upon a giant lotus flower and then diving into the water from it. Visualising it thus, links two things you know — the name and the meaning — in a memorable action.

More examples of how you can use absurd-action visuals, bolstered whenever possible by sound effects, to help you remember names.

Name	Meaning	Absurd-action visual
Pallavi	first musical note in Indian classical music	Several musical notes running a marathon, with the person introduced reaching the finishing line first! Crowd chanting: 'Pallavi first! Pallavi first!'
Purnima	full moon	Person sitting on a full moon which is running about the sky on tiny legs, yelling, 'Get off me, Purnima!'
Gulab	rose	A giant rose putting the person into a flower vase filled with water. Person going; 'Ggg ... Gulab!'
Kisan	famous brand name: Kissan Tomato Ketchup	The person dancing atop a giant bottle of Kissan Tomato Ketchup
Kirschbaum	cherry tree (in German)	As the person flies over a giant cherry tree, the cherries attack him in an explosive burst. The bombardment is accompanied by sound: 'Kirsch! Baum!'

The phonetic emphasis and the absurd drama contributed by the sound effects not only add the fizz that helps to fix the name in your mind, but they also help to fix the *correct* name. For instance, in the examples above, you know that the name is Purnima, not Moon; or Gulab, not Rose!

Practise this method with the names of friends and relatives. It will enhance your expertise in using absurd-association as a powerful memory aid.

Try a Spot of Silly Substitution. This method is really an extension of the absurd-association method. It involves breaking up the word phonetically, using similar-sounding words. In other words, *substituting* with a similar word or sound effect, or both.

Let's take Kirschbaum again:

Phonetic break-up: KEY-RRR-SSHH-BOMB!

To remember it better, add the action link: KEY goes RRR! SSHH! It's a BOMB!

Substitution works for a number of reasons. One, you're using a word you're already familiar with. You know — and will remember — BOMB far better than BAUM. Also, BOMB is tangible, BAUM is abstract.

Since names often are abstract words, substituting a name with a similar-sounding *tangible* word makes it simpler to remember. The tangible word also helps you create pictures in your mind. And the addition of an absurd action cements them in your memory. Take the well-known song: 'Chicken in a car, and the car can't go — that's how you spell "CHICAGO"!'

There used to be a cricketer called V. Subramanyam. Since the British commentators couldn't pronounce this tongue-twisting (to them) name, they substituted Subramanyam with Submarine! But I'm sure if they had used silly substitution and combined it with absurd-action visuals, they would have been able to pronounce his real name. For instance, SUBRAMANYAM could have been:

SUBmarine RAces MAN and humbles his YUMble!

I dare anyone *not* to remember Subramanyam after that! (However, in the case of the British commentators, Submarine stuck and became his nickname!).

Let's practise phonetically breaking up some shorter names before we tackle the longer ones. Remember, phonetic break-ups make for easier memorising just as smaller morsels are easier to chew:

PRAKASH

- PRA-KA-SHH!
- PRAying CAt, SHH
- Picture a cat praying and the person saying, SHH!

TAKASHI

- TAK-ASH-HI
- TACKle that ASH, HIt it!
- Picture the person tackling ash in a wrestling competition, then hitting it!

HENDRYX

- HEN-DRY-EGGS
- HEN DRIes EGGS!
- Picture a hen drying eggs with a hair dryer!

SOHRAB

- SOH-RAB
- SOap the RUBber!
- Picture a bar of soap lathering the rubber!

PEKKANEN

- PECK-AN-EN
- PECK AN HEN!
- Picture the person pecking at a hen!

Set out like this, step by step, this may appear to be a lengthy process. In practice, it happens in the snap of a second. Your mind works faster than you realise! Yes, your imagination does have to be brought into play. But that doesn't call for any new learning or skills. You've been using your imagination all your life. You've only drawing on it now a little more than you normally do.

Ready now for longer names? Here goes:

JAMALABAD

- JAM-ALA-BAD
- This JAM needs an ALArm real BAD!
- Picture a jam bottle waking up with a start as the alarm goes off!

VENKATCHALLAM

- WHEN-CUT-CH-ALUM
- WHEN you CUT your CHum, you get ALUM!
- Picture cutting your chum and finding a piece of alum!

PARTHRAPRAVARTHAKA

- PAR-THRA-PRA-VAR-THA-KA
- PARrot THRives on PRAise, WAR and crows, THA-KA-ka!
- Picture a parrot preening at a war scene and crowing, 'Tha-ka-ka!'

GRIGORYEVICH

- GRIGORY-E-VICH
- GREGORY peck, A WITCH?
- Picture Gregory Peck dressed as a witch!

All this may seem to involve a great deal of creative churning as you rack those little grey cells in the effort to first break up a longish name into snips and then mould these bits into a memorable word-picture. But, believe me, this only appears to be so because you're looking here at examples which I have devised and which work for me. When *you* devise your own, you'll find it's as easy as one-two-three because your visuals will spring from your own associations, using words you are familiar with. And what *you* create will be best remembered by you.

Use the Sounds of Music. Music has qualities that make it an excellent medium for learning and remembering. It stirs the emotions and evokes nostalgia. Many couples who have spent a wonderful evening together in their youth, an evening made memorable by, say, one song that they played over and over on the juke-box, will refer to it many years later as 'our song'. Every culture boasts of a rich oral tradition — whether it's *bhajans*, ballads or nursery rhymes — that served to hand down knowledge from generation to generation. Literate or illiterate, every Indian knows and remembers Krishna's different names — Mohan, Gopal, Kanhaiya. They appear in several songs. So do the names, Radha and Meera. Similarly though we generally forget the names of screen characters within a very short while, we can't help remembering that Julie Andrews' name in *The Sound of Music* is Maria. It's that song, of course, that made it unforgettable for us:

'How do you solve a problem like MARIA?
        How do you catch a cloud and pin it down?
How do you find a word that means MARIA?
        A flibbertigibbet, a will-o'-the-wisp, a clown?'

So, use a familiar snatch of music to help fix a stranger's name in your mind! Take one or two lines of a song you know and adapt them so as to incorporate the name you want to remember.

For instance, in Hindi:

1. *'Mera jootha hai Japani!
    Naam hai RAMANI!'*

2. *'Aaja meri gaadi mein bait ja!
    Aaja meri gaadi mein VANAJA!'*

In English:

1. 'Answer me, LORD above
    Just what sin have I been guilty of?'

2. 'Eight days AVEEK
    I l-o-v-e you...!'

To hone your expertise in the 'lyrical memorisation' of names, you can cash in on the popularity of *antaakshri* game as a social pastime. Use this game as a fun way to introducing your guests to one another at a party. Divide them into two groups. Group A chooses a name from among its members. The person named stands up. Group B then sings a song that incorporates the name of this guest in it! You can be sure there'll be no strangers left at your party!

To sum up what you've learnt about filing away names in your memory:

*   Invest a personal meaning into the name.
*   Link the name to that of a famous name/entity — a celebrity, a sacred river, a mountain range, a hit film.
*   Find out the meaning of the name and create a picture around it.
*   Substitute the name with silly words and sound effects and combine these into an absurd-action visual.

For those who get a kick out of interpreting temperaments and personalities on the basis of star signs, the *Workshop Extra* that follows this chapter harnesses your interest to a new purpose: remembering names with the help of the stars!

Workshop Extra

The Birth-sign Special

Star-signs fascinate most people. But even if you're not an avid believer, you might find yourself becoming interested if I tell you that you can empower your memory using birth-signs as a tool. Specifically, it can be a fun way to remember names.

Since most people know at least their own sign but may be a little rusty when it comes to recalling the entire Zodiac, let alone the characteristics of all the birth-signs, we'll start from the very beginning — remembering the signs in order.

This is how you do it: visualise the first birth-sign symbol interacting with the second, the second with the third and so on. Using absurd association, weave a relay story sequence. Fix each visual in the chain in your mind before moving on to the next.

Here are the absurd-link visuals that I developed. You can create your own.

- *Aries* the ram balances Taurus the bull on his horns!
- *Taurus* tumbles down, snorts, and from each nostril spurts out a twin — the *Gemini* duo!
- Twins *Gemini* dance and hop about to avoid thousands of crabs, *Cancers*, scuttling around on the floor!
- Crab *Cancer* flies in the air and lands on lion *Leo's* tail, at which Leo goes, 'EOW! EOW!'
- Lion *Leo* shakes his mane and out of it flies the virgin *Virgo*!
- Virgin *Virgo* lands with a thump on the scales of *Libra*!

- Thrown out of balance, an agitated *Libra* bites the tail of the scorpion, *Scorpio*!
- *Scorpio*, the stung scorpion, scrambles after man-horse *Sagittarius*!
- Man-horse *Sagittarius* shoots an arrow into the sky, which turns into goat *Capricorn*!
- Thirsty goat *Capricorn* tries to drink water from a pond and finds all the water turning into *Aquarius*, the water-bearer, who's squawking, 'AQUA! KWA! KWA!'
- Water bearer *Aquarius* flips and flops on the dry ground and turns into *Pisces*, a flying fish that soars away into the blue!

Go over these action-pictures — or the ones you may have created on your own — until you're familiar with their sequence. When you've perfected your recollection of this action sequence, you'll find you remember the 12 signs of the Zodiac in order: Aries... Taurus... Gemini... Cancer... Leo... Virgo... Libra... Scorpio... Sagittarius... Capricorn... Aquarius... Pisces.

After this, remembering the months corresponding to these signs should pose no problem since they follow the normal sequence. Just remember that the first star-sign, Aries, starts in March — your memory cue here being the alphabets, AR, that are common to both words, ARies and mARch.

You can make it easier for yourself to remember the sign-month links. First, group them on a quarterly basis, thus:

Aries-Taurus-Gemini	:	March to June
Cancer-Leo-Virgo	:	June to September
Libra-Scorpio-Sagittarius	:	September to December
Capricorn-Aquarius-Pisces	:	December to March

Once you've clustered the signs and the months into groups, fine-tuning their break-up becomes logical and simple:

Aries		March to April
Taurus	March - June	April to May
Gemini		May to June
Cancer		June to July
Leo	June - September	July to August
Virgo		August to September
Libra		September to October
Scorpio	September - December	October to November
Sagittarius		November to December
Capricorn		December to January
Aquarius	December - March	January to February
Pisces		February to March

Next, we come to the actual dates. The easiest way to do this is to assign each star-sign an alphabet so that you can then chant out the whole in effortless rhythm:

Aries	-	Taurus	-	Gemini
A	-	A	-	B
Cancer	-	Leo	-	Virgo
C	-	D	-	D
Libra	-	Scorpio	-	Sagittarius
E	-	F	-	F
Capricorn	-	Aquarius	-	Pisces
G	-	H	-	I

See the alphabet grouping without the star-signs. This is how it goes:

A	-	A	-	B
C	-	D	-	D
E	-	F	-	F
G	-	H	-	I

As you chant it aloud, you'll see that the first three lines have double alphabets each: A-A; D-D; F-F. Only the last, that is, the fourth line, has different alphabets.

Practise fixing the star-sign sequence by the absurd-visual association method, the month-wise grouping, and finally the alphabetic chant. When you've got them down pat, your mind should be able to flash out this sequential chart:

A	A	B
Aries	Taurus	Gemini
March-April	April-May	May-June

C	D	D
Cancer	Leo	Virgo
June-July	July-August	August-September

E	F	F
Libra	Scorpio	Sagittarius
September-October	October-November	November-December

G	H	I
Capricorn	Aquarius	Pisces
December-January	January-February	February-March

The alphabet coding, apart from instantly linking each star-sign to its corresponding months, also helps to fix the dates — because each alphabet stands for a particular date span. Thus, 'A' stands for 21 to 20. The complete code goes this way:

A : 21 to 20	B : 21 to 21	C : 22 to 23
D : 24 to 23	E : 24 to 22	F : 23 to 22
G : 23 to 20	H : 21 to 19	I : 20 to 20

If that's got your mind in a crazy whirl, relax! You don't have to memorise those dates as they're listed above. That has just been put down for you to understand the alphabet-number association; and this understanding leads us to the easy way to remember these date spans. Since all the dates (except the last date in the H span) are in the 20s. I've knocked off the first digit, '2', and retained only the second. For instance, A: 21 to 20. Knock off the 2 and you are left with 1 and 0 which is 10. Thus:

A : 1-0 = 10	B : 1-1 = 11	C : 2-3 = 23
D : 4-3 = 43	E : 4-2 = 42	F : 3-2 = 32
G : 3-0 = 30	H : 1-9 = 19	I : 0-0 = 00

Remember that each alphabet corresponds to the same span of dates whichever star-sign it is linked to. Thus, all As are 10, which means they represent dates 21 to 20; all Cs are 23 and represent dates 22 to 23. Get it? That gives you the total picture, then:

A	A	B
Aries	Taurus	Gemini
10	10	11
March-April	April-May	May-June

C	D	D
Cancer	Leo	Virgo
23	43	43
June-July	July-August	August-September

E	F	F
Libra	Scorpio	Sagittarius
42	32	32
September-October	October-November	November-December

G	H	I
Capricorn	Aquarius	Pisces
30	19	00
December-January	January-February	February-March

Memorising just this much to perfection should be enough to enable you to have the entire sequence of star-signs, their corresponding dates and months at your fingertips. But there's an even better, more fun way of remembering these details. All of us relate to the concept of age. So, imagine that each number stands for the age of that particular star-sign. Line up the members of the Zodiac according to their age — from the youngest to the oldest — and here's what you get:

The unborn Pisces	age 00	I
The youngest — Aries and Taurus	age 10	A-A
Gemini is easy — the twin digits	age 11	B
The only teenager — Aquarius	age 19	H
In its early 20s is Cancer	age 23	C
Touching 30 is the lone Capricorn	age 30	G
Just a couple of years older than Capricorn are Sagittarius and Scorpio	age 32	F-
Libra is the second oldest	age 42	E
And, Virgo and Leo are the oldest	age 43	D-D

THE AGE OF AQUARIUS

See how simple it becomes to remember. Someone tells you his sign is Capricorn. Instantly, you know Capricorn is the lone 30-year-old. As the G-30 flashes in your mind, it spells out the sequential months and dates: 23 December to 20 January.

And you have your complete printout: Capricorn: G-30 ... 23 December to 20 January!

With a little practice, your mind will be able to virtually rattle off the sequence for each star sign. Check them out:

A	10	:	Aries	March 21 - April 20
A	10	:	Taurus	April 21 - May 20
B	11	:	Gemini	May 21 - June 21
C	23	:	Cancer	June 22 - July 23
D	43	:	Leo	July 24 - August 23
D	43	:	Virgo	August 24 - September 23
E	42	:	Libra	September 24 - October 22
F	32	:	Scorpio	October 23 - November 22
F	32	:	Sagittarius	November 23 - December 22
G	30	:	Capricorn	December 23 - January 20
H	19	:	Aquarius	January 21 - February 19
I	00	:	Pisces	February 20 - March 20

You'd never have imagined it could be so simple, would you? And, yes, you can make it even easier to remember by weaving in a simple story-like sequence.

In the first group: the two 10-year-olds lead the twins.

In the second group: the 23-year-old leads the two oldest, the 43-year-olds.

In the third group: the second oldest, the 42-year-old, leads the two 32-year-olds.

In the fourth group: the loners: the lone 30-year-old, the lone teenager, the 19-year-old, and the lone unborn, the 00-year-old!

Doesn't that make it amazingly elementary? Do you think you could ever forget star signs and their months and dates as long as you live?

Now let's go further and link the different signs to their distinctive characteristics. For the purpose of this workshop, keeping in mind that many of you may be new to the fascinating world of the Zodiac, I've selected only a few outstanding personality traits for each sign. They are:

Aries	Extremely creative and spiritually inclined; but these traits are not always obvious due to the outgoing, gregarious nature of the Aries-born.
Taurus	Energetic, brisk and bustling, stubborn (as a bull!) and business-minded. Counts the paise and never overspends.
Gemini	Practical, down-to-earth. A warm manner that belies a cool, assessing nature.
Cancer	Independent, hard-working — painstakingly so. Can be generous to a fault.
Leo	Self-confident, flamboyant, possesses leadership qualities.
Virgo	Sensitive (sometimes over — and overtly — sensitive, quick to take offence), understanding, compassionate and empathetic.
Libra	Extremely imaginative (sometimes verging on the fantastic); retreats hurriedly into a shell or backs off to avoid arguments or controversies.
Scorpio	Highly reserved and dignified, relaxes only with a few chosen friends.

Sagittarius	Bold, optimistic, venturesome, but never to the point of foolishness. Pragmatic in outlook.
Capricorn	Veers between being self-sufficient and self-centred. Makes realistic decisions which may hurt near-and-dear ones, but has the surgeon's ability to make a clean and necessary cut — is cruel in order to be kind.
Aquarius	Far-sighted, thoughtful, capable of deep sensitivity, understanding and empathy. Makes a good intermediary between two friends who have fallen out with each other over a misunderstanding.
Pisces	Has a poetic temperament and is responsive to both metaphors and metaphysics. Has a ear for music: even if not into the study or practice of music, can pick out ragas and chords effortlessly.

Study the above characteristics so that you have a set of thumbnail personality profiles for each sign. Practise by checking out how you, your friends, relatives, colleagues and others fit into these slots. If your boss is an Aquarian, is he far-sighted and thoughtful? Does your Piscean friend turn out beautiful verse? Is your Sagittarian sister really bold and optimistic? The purpose of this exercise in matching people known to you with the distinctive traits of each star-sign is to get your mind to respond to these profiles, to establish a mind-set so that when you meet strangers you're already attuned to making the same kind of connection.

Once this kind of mind-set has been established with practice, this is what will happen when you are introduced to a stranger. During the first five minutes, your mind will 'take in' the name and the first impressions of the person. It will seek and find similarities between these first impressions that it has absorbed and the personality profiles of the various star-signs that you already have at your fingertips. The result of this exercise: a rough-and-ready assessment of the stranger that gives you an immediate take-off point for getting to know him better. So, this is how you do it: After the initial courtesies, you can ask, 'Excuse me, but are you a Virgoan?' or whichever other sign you think he fits. He'll answer in the affirmative or negative. But the conversational ball has started rolling on to a more interesting, more informal plane, and it now gains a momentum of its own as you both discuss why you thought he was a Virgoan. If he is responsive — and most people are — you'll get to know the inner person better in those first five to ten minutes than others who talk about the weather, the excellent host or the food.

What you have done is not only to establish instant communication and a basis for a relationship that goes beyond the formal, but you have also, in quick succession, taken five steps to improve the quality of your long-term memory for people. These five steps are:

Recognition. Your knowledge of the chief distinctive characteristics of the star-signs acts as a bridge between you and the stranger. Your getting-to-know-you attitude sets aside the barriers that social niceties and established norms of interaction generally erect between two people meeting for the first time. These can dampen genuine interest in the other person by keeping communication at the level of polite, almost indifferent courtesies. And, minus interest, as we know, recall is generally poor. On the other hand, recognition, as I have described it here, stimulates instant interest and introduces a certain animation into the interaction.

Assimilation. The discussion prompted by your question, 'Excuse me, but are you a ...?' allows your mind to quickly confirm or reject the early impressions it has already recorded about the stranger — and also to add on more information to what it has already absorbed. At this stage of assimilation, it is important that you tack on his name as often as possible in the course of the conversation (without, of course, overdoing it to the point of annoyance). This allows the name to be assimilated into your memory, along with the other information it is absorbing at the same time.

Integration. At this stage, connections are made as you analyse, interpret, appreciate and meld the various bits of information you have absorbed. Parts of the birth-sign profile you already had in your memory jell with the new understanding you are gaining of the particular person you are now interacting with, and both fuse with the name in a new and unique byte of memory.

Retention. Now comes the interesting stage — the one that fixes the name in your mind. Apart from the similarities you may have recognised between the established traits of a birth-sign and the person before you, you now see clearly also the differences. And it's these differences that set this person apart from others you know and make you see him for himself. As

far as his name is concerned, they act as a kind of super-glue, causing it to cleave to your memory over the long term.

Recall. Generally, this is the difficult part. Yes, you have stored away the name along with the psychological profile of the person, but will your memory be able to summon up that name when you meet him the next time? The short answer is, yes. In your brief but focused interaction with the person, you've had a stimulating and thought-provoking discussion which has demanded involvement and concentration on your part. You've introduced his name into the conversation at intervals, which has involved both, recalling it and saying it out loud. At the end of those five to ten minutes, it does not really matter whether he fits perfectly into any psychological profile or not. What matters is that your mind — your memory — has struck a deep chord with his face, his personality, his name. Your know them — and it's a very good bet you'll remember them.

The reason the birth-sign method is so effective is that the Zodiac profiles act as a focal point when you meet a stranger. The profile that you think fits him then becomes a magnetic hook to which other received information — including his name — gets automatically attached. As his name merges with the old and the new personality profiles, it acquires a texture and quality that makes it individualistic and memorable.

Try it out. I think you'll find that it makes an effective — and fascinating — aid to your long-term memory for people!

Chapter : 4

YES, YOU CAN...

Develop an ability for
'instant recall' of faces ... and
the names that go with them

Stamp a stranger's
personality in your memory

Discover your mind's
vast, untapped powers
of concentration

TOOLS YOU'LL USE

'Observation
with Interest'

Facial Cues

Gesture and Smile signals

Listening Skills

Notebook and pen

AND YOU WILL...

Become the expert's
expert at describing and
remembering faces!

How to Remember Faces

....

Cement them forever in
your memory bank!

....

Though most of us have a better memory for faces than for names, some of us do have a poor recall even for faces. And all of us, at some time or the other, have had the experience of being simply unable to 'place' a face.

Is the reason just that some faces are not memorable — and others are? A wit once said, speaking with an obvious if metaphorical sneer about someone he'd met, 'He had the kind of face that, once seen, is never remembered.'

But he was wrong. It is not so much that some people have the kind of faces that are instantly forgettable, but that we remember certain faces better than we do others because, for some reason or the other, we take a particular interest in them. Let me give you an example. At a party, the local Know-It-All whispers excitedly into your ear, 'See that man in the blue suit? He's a multi-millionaire!' You'll immediately jerk your head in his direction and stare at him in fascination.

Now, if the social butterfly were to say to you, 'The guy in the blue T-shirt is our ex-principal's son,' how are you likely to react? You'll probably spare him a casual glance and dismiss him with an equally casual mental shrug: 'Oh'.

There's no question about who you'll remember more! The moral of this social vignette: You must bring the 'multi-millionaire interest' to all your interactions if you want to make them memorable. This involves a shift in your value system, a recognition that every stranger you meet, though he may not be famous or rich or great-looking, is *important in his own right*. Respect him and you'll look on him with interest. You'll 'observe with concentration' ... and you'll remember him.

The importance of 'observing with concentration', as a way to remembering faces better, is underlined in this small true story from a long time ago:

According to Cicero's records, in 500 B.C. a poet named Simonides, while attending a banquet, was called out of the hall to receive a message. While he was out, the building caved in, killing all the merry-makers in the room. Tragically, so mutilated were the bodies that the grieving families were unable to recognise the remains of their loved ones. However, Simondies clearly remembered where each guest had been sitting, and he was therefore able to identify each body according to its location. It was Simonides' ability to 'observe with concentration' that made it possible for the bereaved families to claim the bodies of their loved ones, rather than agonising with doubt for the rest of their lives.

Remember the Person by Remembering the Personality

Observing with concentration is a little like the birth-sign method. In the birth-sign method, you use the psychological profile to remember the name and face of the person. In observing with concentration, you take in not only the physical profile but the entire personality. And this twin approach to observation is, I find, far more effective than trying to remember only the face because, when it comes down to it, the stranger you meet is not just a face but a complete personality.

There are six components of personality and, therefore, of the observation-with-concentration method:

1. The eyes
2. The facial features
3. Distinctive features
4. Gestures
5. Smile and laugh
6. Voice

When you observe each of these aspects with concentration, the entire personality clicks into a harmonious whole in your memory. Then, the next time you meet this person, any one aspect acts as a trigger to your memory, an instant cue to the entire personality.

Let's study the specific kind of characteristics you need to observe in each of these six aspects of personality:

The Eyes

There are three 'observation points' here:

Colour. Brown, black, blue, green, grey, green tinged with brown flecks. Sometimes the pupils are larger and of a different shade from the cornea.

Shape and size. Large, small, slanted upwards or downwards, almond-shaped, hooded.

It is interesting — and important to know — that posture and body language often reflect the expression in the eyes. Thus:

104

Expression	Posture/ Body Language
Alert	A pair of alert eyes is often beady, bordering on the inquisitive.
Dull	Dull eyes hint at the possibility of the person looking older than he actually is — as if he is suffering from some ailment, physical or mental.
Sparkling/ twinkling	A pair of sparkling or twinkling eyes is often accompanied by a head and body inclined towards you in a friendly, trusting manner.
Opaque	An opaque pair suggests a reserved person who appears to be holding back his body and doesn't seem to be even really inclined to shake hands, though he does it courteously enough.
Cool	Cool eyes reflect a low sense of self-esteem — the person's movements are over-controlled, the body is held in a state of unnatural stillness.
Open	Open eyes go with open body language — and a person who may not stick around to talk to you for more than five seconds because he is sought after and also wants to seek out other people.
Calm	A calm-eyed person presents a certain stillness in the body.
Restless	Restless eyes will barely meet your own. Such a person's shoulders and limbs will also be in a state of perpetual, restless motion — as if he can't stand being in one place.
Interested	Interested eyes are ever-changing, flashing myriad mobile expressions accompanied by flaring nostrils, nodding, bending, straightening shoulders, and expressive sounds like 'Tsk, tsk' or exclamations like 'Wow!'
Indifferent	Indifferent eyes are paradoxical — theirs is a 'switched-off' look, interrupted by occasional, tiny "on-off" flickers of interest However, the body language of the person hardly alters during this shift — as if the 'switch-on' is not long enough for the brain to convey the message to the limbs.
Assessing	Assessing eyes that pay particular attention to your dress and appearance may put you off, but this is a person who also assesses himself in much the same way. He'll be well-attired and will reek of an expensive after-shave or cologne.

The Facial Features

These comprise the several range of variations such as the shape and size of the face, the nose, chin, positions and length of ears etc. The facial features are discussed below:

Shape	Features
Face	This can be round, square, narrow and long, triangular, squat or oval.
Nose	The nose may be straight, hooked, pug, sharp and pointed, with bulging nostrils, flared nostrils.
Chin	The chin may be rounded, pointed, blunt, jutting-out, receding, cleft, double.
Ears	These can be floppy ('lop ears'), protruding ('bat ears'), big, small, rounded, pinned back close to the head, with enlarged or droopy ear-lobes.
Lips	They may be full, thin, pursed, wide, small, thick, Cupid's-bow-shaped.
Forehead	This can be broad, narrow, high with a receding hairline, marked by an accentuated widow's peak.

Distinctive Features

Apart from the chief facial features outlined above, there is also a variety of other physical lineaments that can mark a face and make it distinctive. They include:

- Dimples; a beauty spot or other birthmark.
- Forehead wrinkles; laugh lines around the eyes; shadows under the eyes; turkey-gobbler neck folds.
- Long eyelashes; pencil-thin eyebrows; bushy eyebrows; arched eyebrows; eyebrows that almost meet at the centre; eyebrows that are virtually 'not there'.
- Buck teeth; uneven teeth; large teeth; paan-stained teeth; perfect teeth.
- Long hair/short hair; straight hair; wavy hair; curly hair; afro-curly hair; hair worn loose; hair worn in a chignon;

hair worn in plaits; a receding hairline; a bald head.

- Full beard; clean-shaven; salt-and-pepper beard; sideburns that are long, medium or short.
- Pointed goatee-style; handlebar moustache; toothbrush moustache; moustache military moustache.

Age. Though age is not an 'outstanding characteristic', it does serve as a broad pointer because we all carry a mental impression of what a 30- or 40- or 50-year-old looks like.

If your head is whirling by now at the thought of having to take note of and remember all these different and detailed characteristics of the human face, steady on!

Remember, in the first place, what I've already assured you about before — your mind has vast, *untapped* powers, far more than you can imagine. Secondly, the purpose of listing all these various facial features is not because you need to observe them all, but only to draw your attention to the fact that such a great variety does exist and is displayed, in varying combinations, to your eyes. If you have hitherto been a casual or careless observer, it is because you neglected to take in the distinctive facial features that were on view when you were introduced to and interacted with a person.

From your point of view, then, the face was 'featureless'. But to observe with concentration means that you should pick out just one or two of the more outstanding features and anchor them in your mind. When you look at a cartoon of a celebrity, why do you easily recognise whom it depicts? Because the cartoonist has selected one or two of that celebrity's most prominent features and exaggerated them. The fact that *you* recognise the celebrity depicted means that you too have sub-consciously observed these distinctive features.

It is by *consciously* cultivating this ability to pick out distinctive facial characteristics that you will enhance your recognition of faces and your ability to remember them. You will be able to remember a person as having, say, 'a long, sad face that seems to have settled into a permanent expression of gloom', or as having, 'pale, kindly eyes that look out from behind horn-rimmed spectacles'.

Practise the art of conscious observation by sitting first with a friend, studying her facial characteristics minutely, and then describing them in as much detail as you can. Check out the shape of her face, the tilt of her chin, the colour of her eyes, the shape and fullness of her lips, her customary expression. You'll probably find yourself noting characteristics you'd never lighted on before.

Practise with other friends, too. Then move on to people like colleagues and relatives, people whom you meet fairly frequently. Finally, move on to strangers you are introduced to. Most people observe clothes, hairstyles, jewellery. Instead, use those same powers of observation on features that matter far more where your recall of persons is concerned.

When you've practised sufficiently, you should be able to describe a person you've just met along these lines:

'The woman is in her mid-30s. She has a longish face, attractive, chiselled jawline and a slender, smooth neck. She has a broad, line-free forehead and her eyebrows have been tweezed into high, thin arches. She has small, brown, close-set eyes. They are bright and beady and her head darts about like a little bird's. She has a straight, sharp nose with flared nostrils. Her cheeks are hollowed, with high cheekbones. She has a mole on her left cheek, quite close to her mouth. She is thin-lipped, and has slightly buck teeth. Her ears are tiny and she wears long ear-rings.'

There, that was easy and painless, wasn't it? A little more practice and you'll be the expert's expert at describing and remembering faces!

Gestures

Often, we remember people chiefly because of some typical, at times quirky, gesture. It could be the way she keeps running a hand through her hair at regular intervals as she talks; or, the way he keeps worrying his tie every two minutes.

The smallest, most apparently insignificant of gestures can often provide valuable insights into a person's psychological make-up and his character. They can then be added to your profile of him. The next time you meet him, along with remembering the outstanding features of his face, you'll also remember him as 'the man who constantly chewed on his glasses'.

Someone who holds his glass with both hands cupping it is unsure of himself and is using the glass as a security blanket. So too a person who holds a briefcase tightly against his chest, or a person who bites his lips.

If he taps his index finger against the glass he is holding, he is a domineering person; if he rubs it against his cheek, he is self-opinionated.

On the other hand, if he rubs his lips or tugs at a ear, he is a trifle helpless. Clasped hands also indicate a defensive attitude.

If the fingertips of both hands meet, forming a triangle, it bespeaks arrogance.

If he takes off his spectacles, it means he feels suddenly pressured. If he chews on an arm of his spectacles, he wishes to reserve his opinion.

If, while standing, he constantly crosses and uncrosses his

legs, it indicates he is not sure you are accepting him, but is still open to establishing a friendship.

These, and a host of other gestures, can be valuable cues which you can use as additional pegs on which to 'hang' your memory of the person's face and name.

Smile and Laugh

It's amazing how, what appears at first sight to be an 'ordinary' face, can be instantly transformed by a smile. I don't mean the polite smile that normally accompanies the courtesies of the introduction — that is more like a trailer to the genuine, kilowatt smile that infuses every muscle of the face and seems to set it in an entirely altered mould, even lighting up the eyes. That full-impact smile can be dazzling, sweet, mischievous, toothy, rueful.

A smile that does not reach the eyes also says something important about the person to you — this is a person to be wary of, for he may not be all that he seems, may not mean all that he says. A touchstone cue to the whole person can be contained in just his smile. As William Lyon Phelps said, 'There is a very simple test by which we can tell good people from bad. If a smile improves a man's face, he is a good man; if a smile disfigures his face, he is a bad man.'

While a smile files itself in your visual memory, a laugh files itself in the data bank of your auditory recall. It can be affable and easy; deep and throaty; an infectious chuckle; a joyful chortle; a mischievous gurgle; a winsome giggle; a malicious snigger; a jolly ho-ho-ho-ho; an explosive outburst.

The Voice

Without consciously being aware of it, we 'tape-record' the voices we hear, their accents and their intonations. It's a kind of primal self-defence reaction, inbred in our psyches since our caveman days, when a rustle in the bush could be a life-or-death matter. Science has found that even the foetus in the womb responds to the sounds of its mother's voice or to soft music. A toddler knows from the slightest inflection in a parent's voice whether daddy or mama is happy or displeased. And so on through life. We revel in sweet tones and respond positively to an assertive voice. The affinity we have for sounds may well be instinctual, for it appears to exist even in animals.

> The great sage, Paramahansa Yogananda, tells an amusing story about the time he used to address gatherings in a chapel at Mount Washington and found that a goat seemed to be attracted to the sound of his voice! 'One day, the goat came trotting in and right up the aisle to me!' he narrates. 'I am sure it didn't know what I was saying, it simply liked to hear my voice!'

We might think that unlike the goat, our attention would be so focused on the words and their meaning that we would not pay much attention to the voice or remember it later. But this is not so. We all know how unforgettable those rich radio voices are, how we instinctively visualise the kind of person 'behind the voice', and how, almost invariably, we make pre-conceived connections such as attaching a deep, booming voice to a tall, well-built male. (And how surprised we are when we later see that person on television and discover that he is, in fact, a tiny man with big, protruding ears!)

In addition to the other physical features, a person's voice can also be an excellent memory cue. If you're a good listener, you'll take in the overall quality of the voice, its distinctive accent, the specific emphasis on syllables drawn from regional roots.

There are several kinds of voices: deep; bass; high-pitched; strained; squeaky; hoarse; smooth; rich and full; hollow.

The tones can be warm; dulcet; reassuring; airy; bright; matter-of-fact; emphatic; uplifting.

The possible range of accents is too extensive to list. But it's their very variety that helps to stamp the stranger's personality in your mind and may even act as a hair-trigger when it comes to recall.

As you will have realised by now, there are several distinguishing facets about a person's physical and psychological make-up that can provide memory cues. Observe — with concentration — as many of these facets as you can. What you retain will be your own unique composition of the stranger's personality. The next time you meet him, just one or two strains of that composition floating to the surface of your mind will prompt instant recall of who the stranger is.

How to Link the Name to the Face

So far we've assumed that you've met only one stranger. What do you do if you meet five strangers in one evening? Simple. You apply the same methods for remembering the names and faces of each of them. Ah, but here is where you might stumble ... and link a name to the wrong face.

Imagine if, after all your efforts, you end up calling Mr Chitre 'Mr Sheth' — or vice versa!

You need a way to link the face and the name so that they go unmistakably together. This is how you do it: Prefix any descriptive adjective to the name. For instance: bushy-browed Chitre. Hook-nosed Sheth.

I also suggest that you always carry along a notebook and a pen. When you visit the men's or the ladies' room to freshen up, refresh your memory as well: jot down in your notebook the names of the different people you have been introduced to. Writing them down in your own hand invests them with a subtle personal touch that aids recall. It is also a review: to write them down, you have to first think about them and remember them. It's likely that you'll remember the faces more easily than the names. Writing down the names automatically brings the faces to mind.

Keep your written record. Refer to it every three days or so — this will serve as a 'refresher course'. The next time you meet one of the persons you were introduced to that evening, the name and face will click instantly in your mind and you'll greet him without hesitation.

You may well wonder: is it worth going through all this just to remember a stranger's name and face? It is — not only are you saving yourself the embarrassment of fumbling over people's names (or even trying to avoid some people when you realise you've clearly forgotten their names), but you are creating for yourself a network of goodwill and friendships. You are also enhancing your powers of observation — which will stand you in good stead in other areas of your life as well.

Reputations are often built on this 'taking-the-trouble-to remember' image. I know of several instances that illustrate what I mean. Once will suffice here. A woman I know spent almost an hour talking with a doctor, a renowned cardiologist.

So impressed was she that she decided to consult him if ever she had the need for such a specialist. But when she actually did, confident of the old rapport, she was destined to be disappointed. The good doctor simply did not remember her! She never consulted him again. It was not a matter of 'ego'. But, she explained to me, 'If he doesn't think people are worth remembering, he won't truly care about his patients. When he told me I needed a bypass, I wasn't sure whether I really needed one, or whether I was just one more faceless patient to be dealt with quickly and efficiently on the assembly line. I was not a person to him — only an organ.' Sure enough, when she got a second opinion, she was advised a take-care regime of diet control, yoga workouts, and relaxation techniques. 'I'm glad I listened to my intuition,' she said.

That kind of reaction is common. Rich or poor, young or old, woman or man, we are all sensitive souls in the end — and simple at heart. If a stranger we've met just once remembers us, we are willing to go that extra mile for him. It's exactly what I began this chapter with. Remembering shows a respect for personhood.

Chapter 5

YES, YOU CAN...

Develop 'auto recall' of any telephone number

Even remember any cell phone number you need to!

TOOLS YOU'LL USE

The grouping method

The rhyming method

AND YOU WILL...

Wonder why you used to have such a problem remembering telephone numbers before!

How to Remember Telephone Numbers

It's as easy as one, two, three!

Mobile phones are intended to enhance communication and to make life easier. Even so, you need to remember the cell phone number in the first place! Not everyone has a telephone with a number-storage facility. So, it's back once again to that Old Reliable, your Memory! To make it super-reliable in terms of telephone-number recall, I bring you two simple methods in this chapter: the grouping method, and the rhyming method. You can select either or both, depending on your individual preference.

This is not to say that you *need* to remember every telephone number in your book. Some people do take pride in remembering every possible number. Others prefer to remember only a few important numbers. *You* decide what you'd like to do.

The Grouping Method

To my mind, the best way to remember a telephone number is to simply learn it by heart. Does that sound surprising? It should not. We've grown up learning to chant numbers in sequence, to recite arithmetic tables. We have a certain numeral-rhythm *already* established in our sub-conscious. It is this rhythm that you take advantage of when you want to commit a telephone number to memory.

For instance, let's take a seven digit telephone number: 6364718. Say it out loud without pausing: six-three-six-four-seven-one-eight. Did you hear that hint of a chant in your voice? That's what I'm talking about!

The best way to remember the number is to break it down. All telephone numbers begin with the exchange-area code. That is, the initial digits represent the local area to which the telephone numbers exchange is connected. Thus, 636 may be the Andheri exchange-code in the city of Mumbai. If you live in Mumbai, you should find it even easier to remember: if a person resides or works in Andheri West, his exchange number will be 636, 637, 629, or 631.

Once you've fixed the exchange-code number in your memory, remembering the rest of the digits is easy because there are now fewer of them. The best break-up in terms of rhythm is: 636-47-18. Or, six-three-six (*pause*) four-seven (*pause*) one-eight.

Even if you are not familiar with the area exchange-codes in a particular city, you can still remember the telephone number by breaking it down into three groups. So, a seven-digit number like 6364718 can be broken down into:

1	2	3
636	47	18

A longer number will require to be broken down into more groupings. For instance, 2963452561 is a ten-digit number. So, break it down thus:

1	2	3	4
296	345	25	61

To fix the number in your long-term memory, the principle is a simple one: the more often you dial the number, the more securely it will moor itself in your memory. This is of course the reason you remember the telephone numbers of people you are regularly in touch with, such as your best friend or your business colleagues. However, though you do not call up your doctor every day — nor would you want to! — if you still would like to remember his number, there's a simple step you can take. Buy yourself a toy telephone. Every day, dial (or press) the numbers you would like to remember. Soon you will be able to reel off your doctor's number with pretty much the same ease that you can rattle off your best friend's.

Why does the grouping method work for telephone number recall? It is because of the human ability (and tendency) to group things. Grouping is a basic proclivity of our thinking processes — and, as we group, we generalise. For instance, we know that

all two-footed beings are human, and we therefore make this generalisation. Similarly, we group all four-footed creatures as animals. Culture and history also determine the way we group people. Thus, we categorise Eskimos as people who eat fish. In the West, all Indians are commonly thought of as vegetarians. These beliefs may be right or wrong, but that is not the point here. The point is this human ability to group things, an ability that we can exploit to remember telephone numbers!

So, to summarise the grouping method:

- Break up the number into groups.
- Repeat it aloud in the group format, with pauses to establish the rhythm in your mind.
- Dial it daily to fix it in your memory.

(Sometimes, you may not need the third step at all. The split-group chanting may be sufficient to fix the number in your mind.)

The Rhyming Method

Some people are ill at ease with numbers. But they are comfortable with words. If you are one of them, you can use my rhyming method instead of the grouping system. It's childlike and taps into your sense of fun if you enjoy sing-song verse. As in the grouping method, this one also draws on rhythm, though the emphasis here is on the *rhyme*.

What I've done is to rhyme every number with a word. My ditty is adapted from a nursery rhyme. Remember this one?

One-two, buckle my shoe,
    Three-four, shut the door,
Five-six, pick up sticks,
    Seven-eight, lay them straight,
Nine-ten, a big fat hen!

My verse does not contain lines such as 'buckle my shoe', since that is not necessary to the rhyming method of recall and may even complicate the process! But, as you'll see, each number rhymes with a word. The purpose is simply to create a chant and to have you remember it:

One a sun	Two a shoe	SUN SHOE HIVE
Three a tree	Four a door	
Five a hive	Six a stick	
Seven a heaven	Eight a gate	
Nine a line	Zero a hero	

Now, how do you apply this rhyme to remembering a telephone number? Let's take 6364718 once again. This is how you use my rhyme in tune with the basic chant that goes:

Six-three-six (pause)	Four-seven (pause)	One-eight
Stick-tree-stick (pause)	Door-heaven (pause)	Sun-gate

Or, take the longer number: 296 345 25 61

1
Two-nine-six (*pause*)
Shoe-line-stick (*pause*)

2
Three-four-five (*pause*)
Tree-door-hive (*pause*)

3
Two-five (*pause*)
Shoe-hive (*pause*)

4
Six-one
Stick-sun

Eventually, because of the *exact* rhyming of word and number, the words themselves will fade from your mind, but the numbers will be retained.

I have used, in my rhyme, simple words which are familiar to us all. Still, if you feel more at home with a line such as, 'One a bun', do use it. Just remember to use only *concrete* words in your rhyme, not abstract ones. A tangible item allows you to visualise a picture and allows your mind to get a grasp on it. This is not possible if you use a line such as, 'Three's a free'. How do you visualise 'a free'?

The methods I've described for remembering telephone numbers may seem almost too elementary. And they are. The important thing is, they work! And that is why I know that after you've practised using them, you'll find yourself wondering why on earth you used to have such a problem remembering telephone numbers before!

Chapter : 6

YES, YOU CAN...

Remember dates, formulae, equations, pin codes, prices...

Use one, and only one, system to remember all these numbers and more

Enthral and amaze others with your numerical wizardry

TOOLS YOU'LL USE

The Alphabet code

The Nursery-rhyme code

Absurd Association

AND YOU WILL...

Remember any number you need to, for as long as you want to!

Memorise the longest number in the world!

....
Just 'sound off' your secret
digital code!
....

N ow that we are into numbers, let us explore the world of digits a little more. The method of recall I'm about to describe is unique, a major breakthrough in Memory Land. It involves the use of sounds to remember any number you would like to!

The sounds are similar to the ones you will be familiar with if you have studied a language, such as Hindi or Marathi, that uses the Devnagiri script ... *ka, kha, ga, gha*. All you need to do is

remember which number represents which sounds. And it's easy because you have to remember only ten numbers. Yes, only ten numbers! And they are numbers you already know in the right sequence: 1, 2, 3, 4, 5, 6, 7, 8, 9, 0! See, you are already half-way there!

Now let's see which number represents which sounds in this memory method:

No.	Consonant	Consonant Sounds
1	T	ta, taa, ti, tee, to, too, tay, tie, toe, tao, tue
	TH	tha, thaa, thi, thee, thay, thigh, tho, thou, thue
	D	da, daa, di, dee, do, doo, day, die, doe, dow, due
2	N	na, naa, ni, nee, noo, nay, nigh, no, now, new
3	M	ma, maa, mi, mee, moo, may, my, moe, mow, mew
4	R	ra, raa, ri, ree, roo, ray, rye, roe, rou, rue
5	L	la, laa, li, lee, loo, lay, lie, loe, lou, lieu
6	J	ja, jaa, ji, jee, joo, jay, jie, joe, jou, jue
	SH	sha, shaa, she, shee, shoe, shay, shy, show, shue
	CH	cha, chaa, chi, chee, chu, choo, chay, chie, cho, chou, chew
7	K & Q	ka, kaa, ki, key, koo, kay, kie, koe, cow, cue
	G	ga, gaa, gi, gee, goo, gay, guy, go, gow, gue
8	F	fa, faa, fi, fee, fu, foo, fay, fie, foe, foe, fou, few
	V	va, vaa, vi, vee, vu, woo, way, why, woe, vow, view
9	P	pa, paa, pi, pea, pu, pooh, pay, pie, poe, pow, pew
	B	ba, baa, bi, bee, bu, boo, bay, bye, boe, bow, bue
0	Z	za, zaa, zi, zee, zu, zoo, zay, zie, zoe, zou, zue
	S	sa, saa, si, see, su, soo, say, sigh, soe, sou, sue

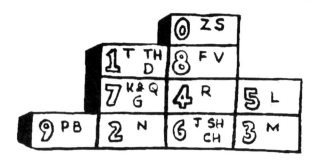

The Number-Sound Code Explained

Of course, the first thing that disturbs your sense of phonetic logic here is that the sound of '1', pronounced 'one', has nothing remotely to do with sounds like 'ta', 'taa' and 'da'! Why on earth did our mnemonics experts say that '1 is for ta, taa, da, 2 is for na, 3 is for ma,' and so on?

Let me explain the process by which they arrived at this number-sound code:

First, they took the 10 digits in our numeric system — 1, 2, 3, 4, 5, 6, 7, 8, 9, 0.

Next, they decided to take ten *basic* sounds and link them to these ten digits. To simplify the code, they decided to take only the consonant sounds such as T (ta), D (da), N (na), M (ma) and so on. They did not take the vowels, a,e,i,o,u, as separate sounds, but as affixed to the consonants.

Their next step was to group similar sounding consonants together. To do this, they had to set aside the alphabet sequence as we know it, A-B-C-D, and instead group together alphabets with similar sounds — just as we do in Devnagiri: *ka, kha, ga, gha... cha, chha, ja, jha...* So:

- T and D are formed by using your tongue against your palate in the same way — as, for instance, when you say, ta or da.
- Ja, sh, ch are articulated in the same way.
- So are fa, ph, and va, wa.
- As are ca, ga.
- Pa and ba.

• And, finally, za and sa.

Having managed this neat grouping of speech sounds, the experts next worked on *linking* the ten sound groups to the ten numbers! The way they did this was by using visual logic. That is, if an alphabet bore a visual/logical resemblance to a number, that alphabet was linked to that number in the memory code. (The exception was '4-R', but here, too, a form of logic was employed.)

So, these are the visual connections that they made to give us the complete number-sound code:

Number	Resembles
1	T ... because T is visually like 1, a vertical line. Or, T is 1 balancing a stick horizontally on its head: T
2	N ... because a small 'n' has two vertical lines which balance a curved stick on their head: TT
3	M ... because a small 'm' has three vertical lines which balance two curved sticks on their head: TTT
4	R ... because the word 'fouR' ends with R or a 'ra' sound.
5	L ... because when you spread your five fingers with the thumb pointing straight out, the thumb and forefinger form an L. Also, the Roman numeral, L, denotes 50.
6	J ... because the capital J looks somewhat like the mirror image of 6.
7	K ... because the capital K looks like two 7s written back to back, and leaning one against the other:
8	F ... because the small 'f', when written in running hand, appears to be an 8 — with two loops and a belt at its midriff:
9	P ... because the letter P is the mirror image of 9.
0	Z ... because 'z' is the first alphabet of zero, which we already know is 0.

Now that you've understood the links and how they evolved, let me lay out the code for you, completely and concisely.

The Number-Sound-Alphabet Table

Number	Sound	Alphabet
1	Ta, Tha	T
	Da	D
2	Na	N
3	Ma	M
4	Ra	R
5	La	L
6	Ja, Sh, Ch	J
7	Ka, Ga	K
8	Fa, Pha	F
	Va, Wa	V
9	Pa	P
	Ba	B
10	Za, Sa	Z

Now that you have a pretty clear grasp of the code, all you need to do to fix it indelibly in your memory is to learn it in a sing-song style, the way you chanted those arithmetic tables back in school. How did they go? Phonetically, like this:

Two one za two (2 x 1 = 2)

Two two za four (2 x 2 = 4)

Two three za six (2 x 3 = 6)...

So, learn the number-sound code the same way:

One T za Ta

Two N za Na

Three M za Ma

Four R za Ra

Five L za La

Six J za Ja

Seven K za Ka
    Eight F za Fa
Nine P za Pa
    Zero Z za Za

You don't need to learn all the sounds associated with each number. For instance, you don't need to chant 'One T za Ta ... Tha ... Da ...'. Just knowing that 1 is T acts simultaneously as a trigger cue to Tha and Da.

Or, if you've always hated those arithmetic tables and can't stomach the thought of going back down that particular memory lane, there's another way to learn the code: the rhyming way, as in 'One, two, buckle my shoe'.

The number-sound nursery rhyme code

One tickled his Toe!
    Two neighed No!
Three muttered Me?
    Four roared Risky!
Five lathered La, La,
    Six jogged to Java!
Seven kissed the Key,
    Eight fumed Fo Fum Fee!
Nine posted the Pip,
    Zero zipped his Zip!

Notice how I've deliberately used action verbs as well as objects beginning with the relevant alphabet. So, it is:

One **T**ickled his **T**oe!
    Two **N**eighed **N**o!
Three muttered **M**e? ... and so on.

This helps you to better remember which number represents which alphabet.

Important: Make sure you know the number-sound system by heart before you proceed to the next stage, which is learning to use this system as a memory aid. If you don't, it's quite likely that you will get confused and lose interest in this method. Remember, it took you days to master the alphabets back in your childhood. Spend a similar amount of time getting the number-sound system down pat.

Let me sum up its main features:
- The vowels *a, e, i, o, u* have no numerical value. Neither do the consonants *h* and *y*. They tend to get absorbed in, or hyphenated by, the ten dominant consonant sounds given above.
- Silent consonants like *k* in knee or knock don't count as *k*. They are part of the na family. For instance, knee is pronounced *nee*, so would be represented by 2.
- Double consonants such as *tt* would still be counted as a single T or 1 because the sound of tt is still T.
- Double letters pronounced differently, count as different individual sounds. For instance, 'accent' would be pronounced as 'aksent', and 'ks' would be represented by two numbers.
- The sound of *x* varies in different words. In xylophone, it is the *z* sound, so gets the numerical equivalent of zero. In fox, it has the *ks* sound, so it gets the numerical values of *k* and *s*, i.e. 70.
- Q, which sounds like *k*, is similarly represented by no. 7.
- When two different letters with the same sound are combined, they are coupled together as having the same single sound. So, *ck* in 'back' would give the single *ka* sound and would get the single numerical value of 7.

130

Get Set Now for Some Net Practice!

You're ready now to put the number-sound code to use in actual memorising. In the initial stages, if you feel the need, you can still keep the table with you for easy reference. Later, you won't need it as you become a master memoriser! Right now let's take some simple examples:

Example 1: Let us look at the number 1. It has the alphabetical sound, T, assigned to it. 1 = T. Now let us take graded steps:
Step 1: Take TEA, a one-syllable word. The sound is a single T. How would you represent it numerically? With the number for the T sound, that is, with 1 — just as for the letter T. So, TEA = 1.
Step 2: Let's now stretch it to a two-syllable word: TEASE. How does that sound? TEE-ZZ. So, (T =1) and (Z = 0). Therefore, TEEZZ = 10. Get it?

Example 2: Let us look at the number 2. It has the alphabetical sound N assigned to it. 2 = N.

Take the word, NET. How do you represent it numerically? The sound of N = 2. The sound of T = 1. So, (N = 2) + (T = 1) = NT. Now insert the vowel sound and you get NET. If you insert other vowel sounds, you can also get KNOT or NUT.

What have we learned so far? That:
Tea = 1
Tease = 10
Net, Nut, Knot = 21

Now see it the other way round:
1 = Tea
10 = Tease
21= Nt = Net, Nut, Knot

Since you're still at the toddling stage of this new memory system, first make sure you've grasped this simple principle well: Since the number-sound system has no vowels, it gives you only consonant sounds; *so, each number can represent different words depending on the vowel sounds inserted.*

See how one number can give you different-sounding words:

Number	Equivalent Words	Other equivalent words
	Vowel sound follows consonant	Vowel sound precedes consonant
1	tea, tie, toe, too, dee, die, doe, do	at, eat, ought add, odd, id
2	neigh, knee, nigh, know, no, now, Noah	an, in, on, 'un
3	ma, me, may, my, moo	am, I'm, om
4	ray, rye, wry, row, rue	or, oar
5	law, lee, lo	awl, owl
6	jay, Joe, Jew she, shoe, show, shy chew, chai, chow	age ash etch
7	Kay, key, coup	eke
8	fee, foe, few, fie	of, if, off
	wee, why, woe, view	Eve, owe
9	pa, pay, paw, pie, pew	ape
	bee, bye, bow	ebb
10	see, saw, sea, so, sow Zee, zoo	is, yes, as, ass ease, easy

While we are still at the stage of single-sound words, keep practising the number-sound system. It should become second nature to you to transpose numbers into words and words into numbers ... as easy to do as reciting the alphabet or numbers. There are two things you can do to help it jell:

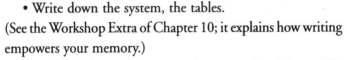

• Write down the system, the tables. (See the Workshop Extra of Chapter 10; it explains how writing empowers your memory.)

• Learn by heart this piece of mnemonic wisdom: *The newcomer's memory requires labour; just keep faith, practise zealously.* Did you get the special message this insightful sentence carries for you? Yes, it is not just a bit of wisdom, it's your instant guide to the alphabets (or sounds) of the numbers-sound code. Read it again: **T**he **N**ewcomer's **M**emory **R**equires **L**abour; **J**ust **K**eep **F**aith, **P**ractise **Z**ealously! You'll see that the first letters of this sentence give you the sounds corresponding to the numbers from 1 to 0 — in their correct sequence!

Once you've mastered the system with single-sound words, you'll find it much easier to move on to double-sound words. In the practice exercise below, I've provided you with just one word per numeral. I would like you to add on your own to hone your memory skills.

Refer to the number-sound system off and on to keep a check on your accuracy.

No.	My Word	Your Word	No.	My Word	Your Word
11	Tot		41	Rut	
12	Tune		42	Wren	
13	Dome		43	Ram	
14	Door		44	Roar	
15	Tail		45	Reel	
16	Deejay		46	Rush	
17	Tag		47	Rag	
18	Deaf		48	Rough	
19	Tape		49	Rub	
20	Nose		50	Lies	
21	Knit		51	Laud	
22	Noon		52	Lion	
23	Name		53	Lame	
24	Neuro		54	Leer	
25	Null		55	Loll	
26	Nudge		56	Lash	
27	Enough		57	Luke	
28	Knife		58	Lava	
29	Nib		59	Lip	
30	Maze		60	Jazz	
31	Mutt		61	Jot	
32	Money		62	Shin	
33	Mummy		63	Chime	
34	More		64	Jeer	
35	E-mail		65	Shell	
36	Match		66	Josh	
37	Amok		67	Shock	
38	Movie		68	Chafe	
39	Map		69	Chap	
40	Rose		70	Geese	

No.	My Word	Your Word	No.	My Word	Your Word
71	Kid		86	Watch	
72	Con		87	Fake	
73	Game		88	Weave	
74	Car		89	Fab	
75	Gale		90	Buzz	
76	Cash		91	Bet	
77	Gawk		92	Pen	
78	Cough		93	Bum	
79	Cab		94	Para	
80	Fizz		95	Ball	
81	Fit		96	Batch	
82	Van		97	Pick	
83	Fame		98	Poof	
84	Win		99	Puff	
85	Fall		100	Dossiers	

Words to Numbers, Numbers to Words

Initially, even after you've mastered the system, you may find it easier to transpose a word into a number than a number into a word. The best way to get past this little hitch is to master the words-to-numbers transposition first. Get entirely familiar with it. Once you do, the numbers-to-words makeover will also become easy. This is how you go about building up the words-to-numbers expertise that you need.

You will have seen a good number of people going off to work every morning with a newspaper rolled up under their arm or tucked into a briefcase. As soon as they are seated, they spread open the paper, get out a pen, and bend their heads over a crossword puzzle. You, too, can while away the commute to work with a mental game, except that yours is a different one — transposing words into numbers and numbers into words.

See how we've taken two headlines from a newspaper and converted their phonetic sounds into numbers:

Foreign	Media	Is	Creating	Panic
842	31	0	7417	927
Proxy	War	Will	Be	Quelled
940	84	85	9	751

It's simple and it's convenient: you simply select headlines and you 'commute' the numbers into words. Before you know it, you'll be a transposing expert!

How to Remember Those L-O-N-G Numbers!

Now that you can transpose words into numbers with speed, let's get down to what the headline of this chapter promised you: remembering a long number. To do that, you work the flip side of the number-sound system: transpose numbers into words. This is a two-way process. First, note the phonetic sounds that

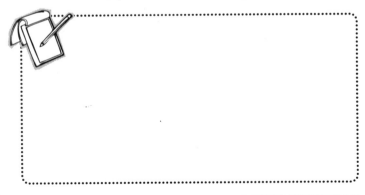

the number represents. Second, add in vowel sound before, between and after these phonetic sounds until you get a *tangible* word (that is, a word that you can create a visual with — it should not be an abstract word).

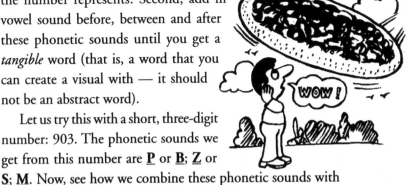

Let us try this with a short, three-digit number: 903. The phonetic sounds we get from this number are **P** or **B**; **Z** or **S**; **M**. Now, see how we combine these phonetic sounds with a variety of vowels to try and get a tangible word:

Pazam; Pezam; Peesam; Possum...
Ah, a *tangible* word — Possum. You can *see* a possum.

On the other hand, it might be easier for you to work with a word like Pizzam. You can definitely picture a pizza! To include the 'm' sound for the digit, 3, you can picture a pizzamma — the mother of all pizzas! As you can see, it sounds silly, there's no word like Pizzamma. Yet, precisely *because it* is so absurd, you'll remember it! A mother 'pizzamma' is also a visual you can easily conjure up, and when you transpose that word into numbers, you'll come up rightaway with the number you need: 903.

However silly a word may sound, don't let it put you off. Remember, *you* are the creator, the boss. You decide which word evokes a picture that's vivid enough for you to remember it — and therefore the number! If your locker number is 903, and Pizzamma's the word that summons up an unforgettable picture in your mind, then Pizzamma's the word for *you!*

Now, let's take that bull (the LONG number) by the horns. Because of computerisation, our bank accounts these days are such a long string of digits that you feel only a computer would be able to recall them! But *you* can too — by using your number-sound memory code! Let's say your bank account number is 9106384574192. Whew, you'll exclaim, that's *thirteen* digits, how ever will I remember them all? Here's how:

Normally, it's already broken up for you. This is how it reads: 910-63-845741-92. If it isn't broken up, do it: group the numbers according to your own breaks.

So let's lay out these grouped digits, along with their corresponding alphabets:

910 – 63 – 845741 – 92
BTS-JM-FRLLKRT-BN

Now insert vowel sounds into these alphabet groupings to form tangible words:

BATS-JAM-FRILLCART-BUN

The next step: use that good old chain-association method that you will be proficient in by now if you have been practising it in earnest. Build your chain of absurd visuals using the tangible words you've created: Thousands of gigantic cricket BATS use JAM bottles as balls. Each time they strike the jam bottles, the jam bottles go for a sixer. Imagine this crazy scenario. Fix it firmly in your mind. Now move on.

An aggressive looking jam bottle boxes with the FRILLCART in a boxing ring. See that little boxing-gloved toughie going

POW! and once again, POW! at the frillcart, which is now on the ropes, its rows of frills entangled in the ropes. And yet the jam bottle keeps punching away at it until it's sliding down the ropes. Are you likely to forget this action-oriented visual? Not likely! Fix it in your mind and move on ...

A hungry frillcart is using its frills as many tongues to lick a giant BUN! This is so ticklish for the bun that it's rolling around in helpless laughter! But the frillcart, with no let-up, continues frill-licking the hys-terical bun. Imagine that frillcart trundling around on its wheels after the bun, its frills hanging o u t like many tongues and going Slurpp! Slurpp! at the bun which is rolling around in helpless glee and going ho-ho-ho, hee-hee-hee! You'd get a Walt Disney award for that kind of animation!

And now that you've gone through all that visualising, what do you have at the end of it? Four word-pictures made memorable through the chain-association method: BATS, JAM, FRILLCART, BUN.

Their corresponding numbers: 910 63 845741 92

See how the number-sound system and the absurd-association method have combined to enable you to remember your long, 13-digit bank number! They have helped you to convert abstract numbers into items you can visualise in your mind. And with this potent memory system, you can memorise the longest number in the world!

There are any number of practical applications. You'll be able to remember all kinds of information involving numbers … dates, telephone numbers, addresses, post-box numbers, weights, atomic numbers, fashion-design numbers, formulae, equations, statistics, credit-card numbers, pin-code numbers, prices... Your life will become easier because you won't need to keep thumbing through a telephone directory or your own phone/address book. If you're a banking executive, you'll be able to remember the account numbers of all the customers you service. In fact, whatever your area of work, study or interest, you'll be able to use this skill productively because, no matter what reason you have for remembering digits, you apply the same system and the same mental operations!

Besides its practical applications, the number-sound system also makes a fascinating hobby: you can spend those long hours commuting or waiting in queues completely absorbed in this game. At parties or other social occasions, you'll enthral others with your ability to recall all kinds of numerical information with lightning speed and absolute accuracy.

So, let's re-cap all you need to know to become a whiz-kid with numbers:

- Understand the number-sound system.
- Know the number-sound system by heart, that is, which number corresponds to which alphabet and word-sound.
- Practise transposing words into numbers.
- Practise transposing numbers into words.
- Use the number-sound system in conjunction with the absurd-association method.

And remember any number — long or short — for the rest of your life!

Workshop Extra

The Number-square Game

Remember the mnemonic you learned by heart when you were practising the number-sound system: The Newcomer's Memory Requires Labour; Just Keep Faith; Practise Zealously! With this mnemonic nugget working for you, you can devise an array of party games and tricks that will keep your friends entertained as well as in awe of you.

Here is one you can try out: The Nine-Numbered Square Game. But before you get down to playing it, first use the number-sound code to make up your list of basic words. You already know which alphabet-sound stands for which numeral. Now make words out of those alphabet sounds:

Basic Word List

Number-Sound	Basic Word
1 - T	Tiger
2 - N	Nilgai
3 - M	Mule
4 - R	Rat
5 - L	Lion
6 - J	Jackal
7 - K	Kangaroo
8 - F	Fish
9 - P	Pig

Learning this basic word list will not be difficult since you already know that 1 stands for T; from that comes T for TIGER. I've taken a list of animals. You can use another category of your choice, say, parts of the body such as Toe, Nose, Mouth, Rib, Leg, Jaw, Kidney, Finger, Palm.

Now, give your friend paper and pen. Ask him to draw a square with nine smaller squares in it as shown on the right.

Number each square serially as shown.

Now, ask your friend to write in each square a number of his choice, between 20 and 99. Each number should be different. When your friend has done this, this is how his square will look

1	4	7
2	5	8
3	6	9

1 22	4 57	7 52
2 35	5 69	8 79
3 41	6 83	9 91

Now, ask him to call out the numbers in sequence, with a pause between each. It is during these pauses that you will engage in the 'memory trick' that will enable you to remember the number in the particular square. Each time you've done your mental coding and you're ready for the next number, prompt him, 'Go on.'

Thus, he reads:

1: 22	4: 57	7: 52
2: 35	5: 69	8: 79
3: 41	6: 83	9: 91

During each pause, this is what you do:

- You associate the serial number (of a square) with the corresponding word from your Basic List. Thus, 1=TIGER.
- Next, you transpose the number your friend has written inside this square (that is, 22) into its corresponding alphabet sound (NN); and you use a vowel to flesh out this sound into a word — for instance, NUN.

- You then use word association to link the two words together. Thus, you might visualise a NUN sitting astride a tiger!

Similarly:

2 = NILGAI. And, 35: ML = MAIL. Visualise the Nilgai reading his mail!

3 = MULE. And, 41: RT = ROOT. Visualise the mule held firmly to the ground by the roots growing out of his hooves!

4 = RAT. And, 57: LK = LAKE. Visualise the rat swimming in the lake!

After you've done this up to square no. 9, take some time to quickly revise your visuals. And you're ready. You now ask your friend to read out the number in any square and you'll give him his numeral for that square.

For instance, he says, 'Three.' You've associated your Mule with a Root (RT), which is 41. And pat comes your answer: 41! Won't your friend be impressed!

There is another, shorter way to memorise in this Number Square game. During the first phase, you bypass the Number-Sound code. Instead, you remember the serial numbers of the squares by linking them to visuals based on their shapes, or on other references that work for you. For instance:

No.	Visualise
1	An upright Diwali sparkler. Standing upright, it looks like a shining number 1.
2	A swan. Its graceful curved neck looks like a 2.
3	A Trishul. It has 3 prongs.
4	A stool with 4 legs.
5	A star with 5 points. Also, 5-star is a well-known superlative.
6	A baby's curl standing like a 6 on its head!
7	An unfinished Swastika.
8	A fat man or woman. It's also a Housie term.
9	A big spoon which you use to ladle dal.
10	A cricket bat and ball looking like 10!
11	Two grains of rice forming the number 11.
12	The sun at noon.
13	Touching wood to keep bad luck at bay!
14	A pole being hit by a zigzag streak of lightning. With a little stretch of imagination, you can make the zigzag into a streaky 4!
15	A trolley or a pram. The 1 is the bar; the 5 is stuck under it, forming the outline of a wheel.
16	It's 'sweet sixteen', so you can visualise 16 sweets in their shiny wrappers!

With this short-cut method, you have ready references for the serial numbers of the squares, 1 to 16. You only need to use the Number-sound code to memorise the numbers inserted in these squares by your friend.

Games like the 16-Number Square Game are not only a pleasurable pastime, but as you continue playing them you increasingly improve and empower your memory!

Chapter : 7

YES, YOU CAN...

Use the magic of memory to perform amazing card tricks

Acquire a fascinating new hobby

Enhance your brain power even further

TOOLS YOU'LL USE

The Number-sound code

Absurd Imagery

Your own Secret Code

AND YOU WILL...

Pull out one ace after another from your sleeve!

Mind-boggling card tricks for everyone!

They will catapult your memory to 'winning' heights!

While a good memory can help you to become a better bridge player and, in fact, to play a better hand at most card games, not everybody plays card games. However, almost everybody is fascinated by card tricks, and this is realm that engages us in this chapter — pulling out that ace from your sleeve! And, in the process of acquiring a fascinating new hobby, you'll find that you also sharpen your memory skills.

First, a recap to refresh your memory

on what we learnt in the last chapter — a number-sound code that went this way:

Number - Sound Card

Number	Phonetic Equivalent	Key Words From Nursery Rhymes	Mnemonic Sentence
1	T	**T**oe	The
2	N	**N**o	Newcomer's
3	M	**M**e	Memory
4	R	**R**isky	Requires
5	L	**L**a La	Labour;
6	J	**J**ava	Just
7	K	**K**ey	Keep
8	F	**F**ee	Faith
9	P	**P**ip	Practise
0	Z	**Z**ip	Zealously

Before we go on, a little lecture:

You are already master of the number-sound code and you can adapt it not only to remember various kinds of material, but also to perform a number of diverting tricks. So, think now of how you can apply this code to a pack of playing cards. Try and work it out on your own before reading the method I've devised. It may take you some time, but you'll grasp it much better. You'll also develop independent thinking (along with improving your memory).

If you have a pack of cards handy while reading this chapter, you will relate better and faster to the tricks. As you know, there are 52 cards to a pack (not counting the Jokers). They come in four shapes, or 'suits' as they are called — Clubs, Diamonds, Hearts and Spades. Each suit has 13 cards — 10 *number-cards* from Ace (1) to 10, and three *royal cards* — Jack, Queen, King.

First, lay out the four different suits in alphabetical order. This will help you to remember their sequence better:

C – Clubs
D – Diamonds
H – Hearts
S – Spades

Keeping this alphabetical sequence, let us give each suit a corresponding number:

Suits/Shapes	Numbers Cards	Royal Cards
Clubs	10	60
Diamonds	20	70
Hearts	30	80
Spades	40	90

Each number-card has its own digit/s. Ace has 1 pip, Two has 2 pips and so on. So, each number-card from Ace to Nine is valued at 1 to 9 pips. Thus:

Ace – value : 1
Two – value : 2
Three – value : 3, and so on.

The royal cards have no pips, only faces. So, let's give each royal card its own value:

Jack: 2
Queen: 3
King: 4

Also, to make the process simple, card 10 will be given the value of 0 — zero, *not* 10. You'll understand why as we go on.

Further, each card has its own value:

Ace	1	Six	6	Jack	2
Two	2	Seven	7	Queen	3
Three	3	Eight	8	King	4
Four	4	Nine	9		
Five	5	Ten	0		

Clear so far? Now translate each card into a two-digit number in terms of its suit value and its pip value, so that every card is represented by a specific two-digit number. Examples:

The Ace of Clubs has one club pip ... 1
Number-card Clubs has a value of 10
So, the Ace of Clubs is 1+10 = 11

The 2 of Diamonds has two diamond pips ... 2
Number-card Diamonds has a value of 20
So, the 2 of Diamonds is 2+20 = 22

The 3 of Hearts has three heart pips ... 3
Number-card Hearts has a value of 30
So, the 3 of Hearts is 3+30 = 33

The 4 of Spades has four spade pips ... 4
Number-card Spades has a value of 40
So, the 4 of Spades is 4+40 = 44

The Jack of Clubs is valued at 2
Royal card Clubs has a value of 60
So, the Jack of Clubs is 2+60 = 62

Identity Numbers

Cards	Ace (1)	2	3	4	5
Clubs 10/60	11	12	13	14	15
Diamonds 20/70	21	22	23	24	25
Hearts 30/80	31	32	33	34	35
Spades 40/90	41	42	43	44	45

The Queen (of Diamonds) is valued at 3
Royal card Diamonds has a value of 70
So, the Queen of Diamonds is 3+70 = 73

The King (of Hearts) is valued at 4
Royal card Hearts has a value of 80
So, the King of Hearts is 4+80 = 84

Get it? We've worked out a simple system where each card is given its own individual Identity Number — a two-digit number. And the entire table is given on the top.

Before we proceed, make sure you have mastered the conversion of cards into their Identity Numbers. Shuffle a pack of cards. Pick out one random card at a time and translate it into its number.

Once you are adept at this, go on to making words from the Identity Numbers, using the number-sound code which you already know.

Identity Words

Cards	Ace (1)	2	3	4	5
Clubs	Tot	Tan	Tam	Tar	Tail
Diamonds	Net	Nun	Name	Nero	Nail
Hearts	Mat	Man	Mama	Mare	Mail
Spades	Rat	Rain	Ram	Rear	Rail

6	7	8	9	10	Jack	Queen	King
16	17	18	19	10	62	63	64
26	27	28	29	20	72	73	74
36	37	38	39	30	82	83	84
46	47	48	49	40	92	93	94

Examples:

The Ace of Clubs' Identity-Number is 11
(1=T) + (1=T) = TT = TOT

The 5 of Diamonds' Identity-Number is 25
(2=N) + (5=L) = NL = NAIL

The 8 of Hearts' Identity-Number is 38
(3=M) + (8=F) = MF = MUFF

The Jack of Spades' Identity-Number is 92
(9=P) + (2=N) = PN = PIN

You can give each card an Identity Word of your choice. However, I'm giving below Identity Words of my choice so that I can explain the card tricks based on them (see bottom).

Master your list of Identity Words before you go on to the card tricks. During your practice sessions, write down both,

6	7	8	9	10	Jack	Queen	King
Tissue	Tack	Toffee	Tap	Toes	Chain	Chime	Chair
Niche	Neck	Navy	Nap	Nose	Can	Cam	Car
Match	Mike	Muff	Map	Mass	Fan	Fame	Fare
Rash	Rack	Reef	Rope	Race	Bean	Beam	Bar

the Identity Number and the Identity Word, at the bottom of each card. Then cover up the cards and try to recall the Identity Words on your own. Check to see if your word was right.

You now have a permanent Identity Number and Identity Word for each card. So, if you're following the list above, the Jack of Clubs can only mean CHAIN to you and nothing else.

And now for the card tricks. (Tip: Always remove the Jokers from the pack!)

Card trick # 1: Who's Got Which Card?

Do this with a group of six friends — you are the seventh person. Ask one friend to shuffle the cards. Then, ask each person to pick out a card and call out the card he has or show it to you. You then need to make some quick associations:

1. Mr Reddy has the 5 of Hearts.
   The Identity Word for the 5 of Hearts is MAIL.
   Picture Mr Reddy at the post-box, and the postbox throwing out his MAIL at him!

2. Dr Patel has the 10 of Hearts.
   The Identity Word for the 10 of Hearts is MASS.
   Picture Dr Patel drowned in a MASS of patients!

3. Ms Rao has the King of Clubs.
   The Identity Word for the King of Clubs is CHAIR.
   Picture Ms Rao being chased by her CHAIR!

4. Ms Kapoor has the Ace of Spades.
   The Identity Word for the Ace of Spades is RAT.
   Picture Ms Kapoor with a RAT on her head!

5. Ms Fernandes has the 7 of Hearts.
   The Identity Word for the 7 of Hearts is MIKE.
   Imagine Ms Fernandes singing into a MIKE — with MIKE
   Jackson!

6. Mr Azad has the 8 of Clubs.
   The Identity Word for the 8 of Clubs is TOFFEE.
   Imagine Mr Azad's cheeks bulging with the loads of
   TOFFEE he's crammed into his mouth!

Having made your absurd associations, this is the line-up
you'll be able to summon up in a snap:

Mr Reddy ... MAIL ... 5 of Hearts
Dr Patel ... MASS ... 10 of Hearts
Ms Rao ... CHAIR ... King of Clubs
Ms Kapoor ... RAT ... Ace of Spades
Ms Fernandes ... MIKE ... 7 of Hearts
Mr Azad ... TOFFEE ... 8 of Clubs

After you can manage this card trick with six friends, try it
with 10, 12, 14, even more. If you'd prefer to surprise a large
group with this trick, try it first with imaginary 'friends' in the
privacy of your home ... dolls, chairs, souvenirs.

Card trick # 2: Guess the Missing Cards

Shuffle the deck, take out six cards and put them aside without looking at them. Then:

1. Look through the rest of the cards, one by one.
2. Quickly recollect the Identity Word for each card.
3. Associate these words with yourself: say, your toes with tot, tan, tam, and the other 'T' words from the Identity Word list, your mouth with mat, man, mama and the other 'M' words in the list and so on. In our list, we have 10 words each beginning with T, N, M and R, and 3 words each beginning with CH, C, F, and B.
4. As you tick them off, you'll know which Identity Words are missing and identify the missing cards.

From six cards, you can graduate to eight, ten, twelve and more as you master this trick.

Card trick # 3: Guess My Hand

You'll require four persons (besides yourself) for this one. Ask one person to shuffle the cards and to deal them out so that each player gets 13 cards. Have three of the players read out the hands dealt to them. The trick you're going to perform is to guess the cards the fourth person holds.

This is not as mind-bogglingly impossible as it may seem at first! Here's how you do it. Say, the cards held by Sheela, Veena and Farida are:

Sheela	Veena	Farida	Tina
4 of Hearts	6 of Diamonds	5 of Spades	?
8 of Diamonds	5 of Clubs	5 of Diamonds	?
Ace of Spades	Queen of Clubs	Ace of Hearts	?
Jack of Diamonds	3 of Diamonds	7 of Spades	?
4 of Clubs	6 of Hearts	King of Diamonds	?
King of Clubs	Ace of Clubs	Jack of Clubs	?
2 of Diamonds	8 of Spades	Ace of Diamonds	?
10 of Diamonds	Queen of Spades	7 of Hearts	?
10 of Hearts	3 of Hearts	Queen of Hearts	?
2 of Hearts	2 of Spades	King of Spades	?
6 of Clubs	8 of Hearts	2 of Clubs	?
Jack of Hearts	3 of Spades	4 of Spades	?
9 of Diamonds	8 of Clubs	10 of Clubs	?

When Sheela calls out 4 of Hearts, you know it is 34 — MARE. Picture yourself galloping on a giant mare! Next, the 8 of diamonds, which translates into 28 — NAVY. Imagine yourself dancing at the Navy Ball! In this manner, you quickly associate yourself with the Identity Words:

Sheela

4 of Hearts: MARE
8 of Diamonds: NAVY
Ace of Spades: RAT
Jack of Diamonds: CAN
4 of Clubs: TAR
King of Clubs: CHAIR
2 of Diamonds: NUN
10 of Diamonds: NOSE
10 of Hearts: MASS
2 of Hearts: MAN
6 of Clubs: TISSUE
Jack of Hearts: FAN
9 of Diamonds: NAP

Now, do the same with Veena and Farida's hands. Next, run through the entire Identity Word list:

Did I associate TOT with myself? Yes.
Did I associate TAN with myself? Yes.
Did I associate TAM with myself? No.

So you know that Number 13, or the 3 of Clubs, is missing. When you've run through your entire checklist, you'll find that the following Identity Words are missing (and that the respective cards they stand for are therefore with Tina):

TAM: 3 of Clubs
TACK: 7 of Clubs
TAP: 9 of Clubs
NERO: 4 of Diamonds
NECK: 7 of Diamonds
MAIL: 5 of Hearts

MAP: 9 of Hearts
RACE: 10 of Spades
RASH: 6 of Spades
ROPE: 9 of Spades
CAM: Queen of Diamonds
FARE: King of Hearts
BEAN: Jack of Spades

Practise first with only the Royal cards. Then with only the Number cards. Finally, you'll be able to sail through the entire pack.

Also, initially write down the associations. Later, you'll be able to do them all in your mind.

Card trick # 4: Spin off the Sequence

Can the Number-Sound code help you to remember the sequence in which a series of cards has been called out? Certainly, it can! Let's start with six-card sequence. Ask a friend to shuffle a pack and to call out the first six cards. Say, he calls out:

1. Nine of Clubs
2. Jack of Diamonds
3. Five of Clubs

4. Three of Hearts
5. King of Clubs
6. Jack of Clubs

Apply the absurd-association chain method. First, get together the Identity Words for the six cards:

TAP-CAN-TAIL-MAMA-CHAIR-CHAIN

Now, connect these six words, one to the other, using absurd imagery: TAP to CAN, CAN to TAIL, TAIL to MAMA, MAMA to CHAIR, CHAIR to CHAIN.

Then, re-connect the Identity Words with the cards they represent!

Later, you can do this trick using more cards.

Card trick # 5: Read My Mind and I'll Read Yours!

This one's not as easy as the earlier tricks, but it's an excellent memory upper since it gets you to *really* concentrate! The flip side: As your concentration sharpens, your memory gets better and better. So, don't give up on this clincher!

You'll need a cooperative partner, and one who's also familiar with the Number-Sound system. The two of you will evolve your own secret code. And the upshot; you'll appear to your enraptured audience to be reading each other's minds!

The trick you are going to demonstrate is that, as each of you picks a card from the pack, the other will call out that card.

It's important that both of you know the alphabetical sequence of the suits and their numerical values:

Clubs: 1   Diamonds: 2
Hearts: 3   Spades: 4

You now need a code that you will use to signal to your partner the card that you hold. Here is the code that will flash out your secret message: In your prompting sentence to your partner, the first consonant of the first word signals the suit (i.e. the shape), while the first consonant of the second word signals the number of pips.

Thus, if the card held is the 2 of Spades, think of it as:

(Spades = 4) + (2 = 2) = **4 2**.

So, your partner prompts you with a sentence like, 'Ready Now!'

Translation: R = 4; N = 2 according to the Number-Sound code. So, you immediately re-connect:

4 = Spades; N = 2. And you get: The 2 of Spades!

Example 2:   Your partner is holding a card.
He prompts: '**D**on't **F**ail me here!'
You translate: D = 1 = Clubs; F = 8.
And you get: 8 of Clubs!

Example 3:   Your partner is holding a card.
He prompts: '**N**ow, **L**ash out your genius!'
You translate: N = 2 = Diamonds; L = 5.
And you say: 5 of Diamonds!

So, now you have five card-tricks with which to impress, amaze and amuse your family, friends and colleagues. And what's more, pole-vault your memory to dizzying heights!

Chapter : 8

YES, YOU CAN...

Use mnemonics to
take the knight on a
unique journey around
the chessboard

Square off with
a wonderfully-
honed memory!

TOOLS YOU'LL USE

The Number-sound code

A new Nursery Rhyme

AND YOU WILL...

Make some 'memorable'
new moves with a
master strategist!

Develop the Memory of a Chess Champion!

Rhyme-around the board in 34 moves!

As any chess player will tell you, the knight is a strategic piece on the board, a guerrilla who engages in sniper attacks. Though in hierarchy he is just above the humble pawn, in the hands of a master strategist he can be more powerful than the queen!

What we are going to do in this chapter is to chart out a tour of the chessboard for the knight in such a way that he travels over the entire board but lands on each square just once. No, you don't have to be a chess player to ride with this knight. But you'll be completely absorbed and enthralled by the memory system that you'll use to pilot the knight on his journey.

First, one ground rule of chess. The knight can move only two ways:

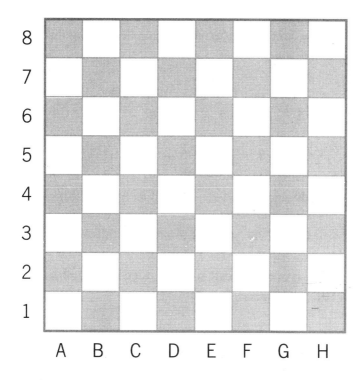

1. two squares vertically plus one horizontally, or
2. two squares horizontally and one vertically. He always glides from a black to a white square, and vice versa.

The squares on a chess-board are lettered vertically, A to H, and numbered horizontally, 1 to 8, as shown in the diagram above.

So, each square has its own letter-number. For instance, D4 is the square where the D column meets the 4 row. Now, take a word that has D as its first letter. Using the Number-Sound Code, translate 4 into R. So D4 becomes DR and you make the word Door or Dare or Deer. Since this system has 8 as its highest number, you can use as many consonants as you like. Just make sure that the alphabets always (as shown in the diagram) precede the numerals. Thus, it should always be D4, never 4D.

Now, for the great secret! The complete tour of the knight goes this way:

A1 — B3 — C1 — E2 — G1 — H3 — G5 — H7
— F8 — D7 — B8 — A6 — B4 — A2 — C3 — B1
— D2 — F3 — E5 — D3 — C5 — A4 — B6 — A8
— C7 — E8 — G7 — H5 — G3 — H1 — F2 — D1
— B2 — C4 — A3 — B5 — A7 — C8 — E7 — G8
— H6 — G4 — H2 — F1 — E3 — F5 — D6 — E4
— F6 — D5 — F4 — E6 — D4 — C6 — A5 — B7
— D8 — F7 — H8 — G6 — H4 — G2 — E1 — C2

You give each square a word, using the Number-Sound Code. For instance:

1	A1 : AT = AT	16	B1 : BT = BUT
2	B3 : BM = BUMBLING	17	D2 : DN = DIN
3	C1 : CT = CAT	18	F3 : FM = FUMED
4	E2 : EN = ENTERED	19	E5 : EL = ELK
5	G1 : GT = GOT	20	D3 : DM = DAME
6	H3 : HM = HYMN	21	C5 : CL = COLOURFUL
7	G5 : GL = GLOWERED	22	A4 : AR = ARCHED
8	H7 : HG = HOG	23	B6 : BSH = BUSHY
9	F8 : FV = FAVOURS	24	A8 : AF = AFFAIR
10	D7 : DG = DOG	25	C7 : CK = COCKY
11	B8 : BF = BUFFALO	26	E8 : EV = EVER
12	A6 : AJ = AGILE	27	G7 : GG = GIGGLE
13	B4 : BR = BEAR	28	H5 : HL = HAILEY
14	A2 : AN = ANNIE	29	G3 : GM = GAMELY
15	C3 : CM = COMICAL	30	H1 : HT = HAT

31	F2 : FN = FUNNY	48	E4 : ER = EARLY
32	D1 : DT = DOTTY	49	F6 : FSH = FISH
33	B2 : BN = BONNY	50	D5 : D6 = DULL
34	C4 : CR = CROWED		
35	A3 : AM = AM	51	F4 : FR = FOREVER
		52	E6 : ECH = EACH
36	B5 : BL = BLACKBIRD	53	D4 : DR = DOORS
37	A7 : AK = ACT	54	C6 : CCH = CHURCH
38	C8 : CF = COFFEE	55	A5 : AL = ALL
39	E7 : EK = EK		
40	G8 : GV = GIVE	56	B7 : BK = BACK
		57	D8 : DF = DEAF
41	H6 : HJ = HEDGEHOG	58	F7 : FK = FAKE
42	G4 : GR = GRATING	59	H8 : HV = HOVERED
43	H2 : HN = HAND	60	G6 : GSH = GOSH
44	F1 : FT = FITTING		
45	E3 : EM = EMBERS	61	H4 : HR = HEARD
		62	G2 : GN = GONE
46	F5 : FL = FLASHED	63	E1 : ET = ETERNITY
47	D6 : DSH = DASHED	64	C2 : CN = CAN

Using these words in sequence, I've made up a memorable nursery rhyme. You can of course make up your own words using the code and your own nursery rhyme.

1. <u>AT</u> dawn, the <u>BUMBLING</u> <u>CAT</u>
    A1   B3   C1
    <u>ENTERED</u> and <u>GOT</u> a <u>HYMN</u>!
      E2   G1   H3
    <u>GLOWERED</u> the <u>HOG</u> at this unfair whim,
      G5   H7
    He owed her no <u>FAVOURS</u>, not him!
                    F8

2. The <u>DOG</u> barked, the <u>BUFFALO</u> bellowed,
      D7   B8

   The <u>AGILE</u> <u>BEAR</u> leapt up in fright!
        A6   B4

   <u>ANNIE</u> laughed at the <u>COMICAL</u> sight,
     A2   C3

   <u>BUT</u> the <u>DIN</u> went on from morn to night!
    B1   D2

3. <u>FUMED</u> the <u>ELK</u>, a <u>DAME</u>
     F3   E5   D3

   With a <u>COLOURFUL</u> nature,
           C5

   <u>ARCHED</u> <u>BUSHY</u> brows her signature,
     A4   B6

   She denounced the <u>AFFAIR</u> as <u>COCKY</u> and tame!
             A8   C7

4. <u>EVER</u> ready for a <u>GIGGLE</u>
    E8   G7

   Was <u>HAILEY</u> the hare
        H5

   <u>GAMELY</u> she spun her <u>HAT</u> in the air!
     G3   H1

   I'm <u>FUNNY</u>, I'm <u>DOTTY</u>, she wiggled!
     F2   D1

5. <u>BONNY</u> <u>CROWED</u> loud and long.
     B2   C4

   'I <u>AM</u> a <u>BLACKBIRD</u>,' said he.
     A3   B5

'I <u>ACT</u> like a crow, am the colour of <u>COFFEE</u>
  A7   C8

Perhaps I'm <u>EK</u>, Do, Teen — right or wrong!'
           E7

6. '<u>GIVE</u> me a smooth skin!'
     G8

Cried the <u>HEDGEHOG</u>, <u>GRATING</u> his quills!
              H6   G4

'On my <u>HAND</u> place some smoothening pills!'
           H2

'It's not <u>FITTING</u>,' sniffed the birds through their bills!
             F1

7. The fiery <u>EMBERS</u> of confusion
            E3

<u>FLASHED</u> and <u>DASHED</u>
  F5   D6

The <u>EARLY</u> worms turned and thrashed
     E4

Even the <u>FISH</u> looked <u>DULL</u> of emotion!
       F6   D5

8. This can't go on <u>FOREVER</u>!
               F4

<u>EACH</u> one said in universal woe
  E6

Open the <u>DOORS</u> of the <u>CHURCH</u>, let us go!
          D4   C6

But <u>ALL</u> sat still, every friend, every foe!
  A5

9. 'I'm <u>BACK!</u>' said the nightingale's sweet tones.
    B7

    Even the <u>DEAF</u> knew, no <u>FAKE</u> was she,
    D8   F7

    They <u>HOVERED</u>, and <u>GOSH!</u> As they <u>HEARD</u> the honey...
    H8   G6   H4

    <u>GONE</u> was their craving for <u>ETERNITY!</u>
    G2   E1

10. To do the best you <u>CAN</u>
                        C2

    Should be everybody's credo: woman or man's

    You'll find that the last square, C2, is so strategic that you
    can move the knight back to A1, the square from which he
    began his journey! This means that you can start from any
    square as long as you follow, in sequence, the cues provided by
    the nursery rhyme.

    Eventually, the moves will fix themselves in your memory
    and you won't even need the nursery rhyme. But if you're ever
    stuck for a move, just recall the ditty and onward rides your
    knight!

Chapter : 9

YES, YOU CAN...

Remember a collection of mixed items/data

Produce order out of confused thinking

Make life easier for yourself and for those you share your space with

TOOLS YOU'LL USE

Filing Systems

Prime-time creativity

AND YOU WILL...

Discover that to be orderly is to learn better, remember more than you ever did before!

Instant Recall through Classification

....
Make remembering the 'order' of the day!
....

Let me narrate to you the story of Manduk, the little frog.

Manduk's Wisdom

Manduk, the little frog, was a BIG dreamer if you considered his size! From the time he was a tiny tadpole, he had heard scary stories about monstrously frightening places like lakes, brooks, rivers, seas, oceans. You see, Manduk belonged to a tiny amphibian population that made its habitat in a pond.

But Manduk was consumed by curiosity. He wanted to find out for himself whether those places he'd heard so much about were really as frightening as they sounded.

So, one day, Manduk began to swim ... He swam and swam and swam. He swam into streams, into brooks, into rivers, into lakes, into waterfalls, into channels, into creeks, into canals, into lochs, into lagoons, into gulfs, into reservoirs, into puddles, into wells, into tributaries, into seas, into oceans. He swam north, he swam south, he swam east, he swam west.

And then, as he swam back home, Manduk was struck by a Great Idea. So excited did it make him and so eager was he to share this Great Idea with his fellow-frogs that he swam faster and faster and faster ...

He reached his pond just as the sun rose in the east. And everybody greeted Manduk, the travelling frog, with great cheerful croaks of welcome! By now, close to bursting with his Great Idea, Manduk shouted joyfully, 'Friends! I have seen everything there is to be seen! I've seen brooks and rivers and lakes and waterfalls and channels and creeks and canals and lochs and lagoons and gulfs and reservoirs and puddles and wells and tributaries and seas and oceans! And do you know something? They are all WATER! Only WATER!'

Thus, due to Manduk's astute thinking, which led him to classify all those 'monstrous' unknowns as water, the fear of every frog in the pond vanished!

So, if ever you are frozen with fear because you feel overwhelmed by a sea of facts, do as Manduk did: CLASSIFY! Whip those facts into order by grouping them. Scientists, librarians, doctors, writers, all successful people in fact, owe a great part of their success to the fact that they classify the information at their disposal.

Classification can also help you in your quest for a super-memory. I'd like you to prove this to yourself with a fun quiz.

Look at the picture below for 60 seconds. Then, cover the picture and try to name all the objects in it. There are 16. Can you name all 16 objects?

You'll find it's pretty tough to recall so many items which have been placed at random about the picture so that they apparently do not share anything in common with one another.

Now, classify them. And what do you get?

See how much simpler it becomes to remember these ordered items now?

Furniture	Fashion Items
Bed	Boots
Desk	Coate
Recliner	Necklace
	Sunglasses
	Handbag

Household Appliances	Fitness/Sports Equipment
Mixer-cum-Grinder	Rowing Machine
Vacuum Cleaner	Ball
Refrigerator	Racquet
Iron	
Microwave Oven	

Now try classifying the objects in the room you are sitting in right now. Group them as we did the objects in the picture above, and you'll find it really becomes easier to remember *more* objects when you club them into categories. As you continue to practise, you'll find you will be able to remember *all* the objects in the room!

Similarly, you can use the classification method to remember almost any kind of information that lends itself to being categorised.

How Should You Group?

How you group people, places or objects depends on your viewpoint and the goal you hope to achieve. For instance, the armed forces will have its classification system based on height, body measurements, physical fitness, education, and so on.

Classification enables you to categorise either into broad groupings or into smaller sub-divisions.

Let's say you want to classify these 18 countries into categories:

China	Indonesia	Nigeria	Nauru
India	Marshall Islands	Bangladesh	Monaco
Japan	Liechtenstein	Vatican City	Brazil
Andorra	Pakistan	USA	San Marino
Tuvalu		Palau	

You can classify them according to their population:

More Than 500 Million:	China
	India
More Than 50 Million:	USA
	Indonesia
	Brazil
	Pakistan
	Japan
	Bangladesh
	Nigeria
More Than 50,000:	Marshall Islands
	Andorra
Below 50,000:	Vatican City
	Nauru
	Tuvalu
	Palau
	San Marino
	Liechtenstein
	Monaco

Another way of classifying them is according to their location:

Asia	Americas	Africa	Europe	Pacific
China	USA	Nigeria	Vatican City	Tuvalu
India	Brazil		Liechtenstein	Nauru
Indonesia			Monaco	Palau
Pakistan			Andorra	Marshall Islands
Japan			San Marino	
Bangladesh				

And you can sum up both classifications to make a concise chart:

	Asia	Americas	Africa	Europe	Pacific
Over 500 million	China India				
Over 50 million	Indonesia Pakistan Japan Bangladesh	USA Brazil	Nigeria		
Over 50,000				Andorra	Marshall Islands
Below 50,000				Vatican City San Marino Liechtenstein	Tuvalu Nauru Palau Monaco

Your mind also sorts through and catalogues millions of bits of information, slotting them into different themes and patterns, and recovering data from these slots to feed to you as and when you need it.

Catalogue Your Personal Library

Filing systems are big business in libraries. Yours is more a part-time affair. But it can bring in the same kind of rewards. If your personal collection of books is threatening to drown you in its sheer volume, I suggest you use the Dewey Decimal System Classification, which most libraries use. In this system, all knowledge available in print is divided into nine main classifications, numbered in hundreds from 100 to 900. The nine classes are:

100 : Philosophy and pscychology
200 : Religion
300 : The Social Sciences
400 : Language
500 : Sciences
600 : Technology
700 : Arts
800 : Literature and Rhetoric
900 : Geography, History and Biography

Each of these categories is further broken down into ten sub-divisions. Thus, Technology (600) is broken down into 610 (Medical Science), 620 (Engineering and Applied Operations), 630 (Agriculture and Agricultural Industries), and so on. General works in each class that don't fit into any of the sub-divisions are grouped into the 000 category which precedes the others. Thus, general works in the Technology category would be grouped in the 600 slot; general works in the Sciences would be grouped in the 500 slot.

Each of these nine sub-divisions can be further broken down if you need a more detailed system of classification. Thus, 620 in the Technology division can be broken up thus:

620	:	Engineering and Applied Operations
621	:	Applied Physics
622	:	Mining and Related Operations
623	:	Military and Naval
624	:	Civil Engineering
625	:	Railways and Highways
626	:	Not Assigned or No Longer Used
627	:	Hydraulic Engineering
628	:	Sanitary and Municipal Engineering
629	:	Other branches

If required, each of these sub-divisions can be even further broken down through the addition of a decimal digit, say: 622.1, 622.2 and so on. (The blank slots, such as 626, enable the addition of new categories as the boundaries of knowledge and scientific discovery advance.)

In the case of your personal library, you probably won't need to go into as extensive cataloguing and as many sub-divisions as a public library. But if you grasp the concept, you'll be able to adapt it to your needs. You'll also be able to add new books as well as new classifications and sub-classifications as and when you need to.

Other classification systems are also in use, such as the alphabetical system, in which a number of keywords — such as *Astronomy, Inventions* and *Explorations* — are first arranged in alphabetical order (as they would be in an encyclopaedia), and subjects are then grouped in these categories, again in alphabetical order. Thus, in the category of *Inventions*, you might group Balloon, Chocolate, Computer, Match-stick, Photography and so on.

However, the alphabetical system has a drawback: if you need comprehensive information on, say, photography, you might have to hunt around quite a bit to find it all since it is likely to be scattered over several categories such as *Inventions, Media, (The) Arts, Hobbies, Technology,* and so on. That is because it is difficult to put under one keyword the various aspects of a particular subject. The Dewey system is the natural popular choice because it uses a *subject-wise* classification; there are no two ways about which category will give you information on, say, General Principles (of Mathematics) (511) or Algebra and Number Theory (512). This avoids confusion and saves time.

To make it even easier to access a particular book you may need, you can adapt a system of labelling that libraries generally make use of. That is, you give each book what is called a *call number,* which determines its location on your bookshelf. You need not get as elaborate as a library system; your label can comprise just two bits of information. The first line of the label states the *classification number* of the book; the second line states the first three initials of the *author.* Thus, using a basic form of the Dewey system, you would label the book, *The Invisible Invaders* by Peter Radetsky, thus:

(610 is the Dewey classification number for 'Medical Science', which itself comes in the technology {600} section. The author of 'The Invisible Invaders', a book on viruses, is the well-known Peter Radetsky). The label is pasted on the spine of the book and the book is then put away on your shelves in the *TECHNOLOGY / Medical Science* section, and in alphabetical order in terms of author's name. This kind of classification enables you to locate it in a matter of seconds.

Classify Your Clippings

If you are a voracious reader and a compulsive collector of information in the form of newspaper and magazine clippings, you can make life easier for yourself and for those you share your home with by devising a simple system for classifying these clippings and retrieving them at a moment's notice when you need to.

Start with a subject-wise grouping. For instance:

Health and Fitness	Law
Environment	Home Appliances
Travel	

Depending on how extensive your collection of clippings in a particular category is, you can then sub-divide. For instance, the *Health and Fitness* category can be broken into: Nutrition, Drugs, Childcare, Fitness Equipment, and so on. However, don't make the classification over-elaborate. That can become self-defeating since it will increase clutter as well as your workload as you struggle to file away your clippings into myriad little slots.

Classify Your Stock-in-Trade

Even the smallest business can benefit from classification because it simplifies procedure and saves time. Let's say you own a chemist's shop. You can stack items on your shelves in these categories:

Babycare Items	**Medical Supplies**
Formula milk powder	Aspirin
Teething rings	Cough drops
Feeding bottles	Bandage rolls
Disposable nappies	Thermometers
	Disinfectants

Cosmetics	**Electrical Appliances**
Lotions/creams	Torch
Talcum/face powders	Electric razor
Perfumes	Electronic mosquito repellents
Lipsticks	Reading lamp
Nail-polish	

Classify Your Work Material

If your work desk is awash in paper — project reports, memos, reference material, notes to yourself — you obviously are in need of paper control. Filing and classifying can come to your aid here too. The basic requirement: to keep on your desk only what is required today or in the near future, and to classify the rest into appropriately-named files for easy recovery as and when you do require them. Even the paper that does stay on your desk or in one of its drawers can be filed away into some kind of organiser with labels such as 'Call', 'Reply', and 'Return'.

Material that you may require on an as-is-needed basis, or in the next week or so, can go into one of your desk drawers or a nearby shelf, but once again into some kind of organiser. Finally, papers that you may require some day, but not very soon, must be filed away too, but kept in a place away from your desk.

Just as you classify clipping, you can also classify visiting cards into categories such as:

Business (suppliers, buyers, and so on)

Hotels and Restaurants

Professionals (doctors, lawyers, and so on forth)

Office maintenance (typewriter/computer service agency)

Friends

Home maintenance (plumber, telephone company, electricity company, etc.)

Vehicle maintenance (mechanic, tyre retailer, etc.)

Classify Your Time

That heading might lead you to the conclusion that I'm suggesting you have a timetable plotting out what you will do every hour. Not at all! I can't think of a more boring way of living. Also, this kind of a time-table only puts you under stress — as if a mental clock is ticking away the seconds and when the time for one task is 'up' you'll have to stop what you're doing and jump ahead to the next task.

What I'm suggesting is something very different. Set aside a few hours each day during which you leave instructions that you are not to be disturbed. Choose the time according to your hours of peak creativity. If your creativity is highest in the early morning, keep aside a few hours for doing your most demanding work at this time. Click on your answering machine and leave a message telling callers what time they should get back to you.

The morning hours are 'prime time' for most people, but far too many people spend half the morning reading the newspapers. Instead, you can optimise your prime time by reading, say, only the front page in the morning and keeping the rest for later in the day when you need to take a breather from work.

By barring interruptions during your peak hours of creativity, you allow your thoughts free rein. Recalling is also easier when you have such 'sacred space' for yourself. The solitude and the quiet help you make reliable associations between the new data and your memory bank, paving the way for storing *more* information and storing it accurately.

But Isn't 'Order' Inimical to Creativity?

In times when we didn't know better, the determinedly bohemian style of our artists and thinkers led us to believe (wrongly) that to be creative is to be disorderly. From that sprang the converse belief: that to be orderly is to be non-creative. Thus, filing and cataloguing and other modes of classification became equated with the lowly clerical orders.

We've come a long way since then. We know today that classification is a primary aid to learning and remembering. It stimulates the thinking process, since to group items or concepts together requires that you think about them and sort them out in the first place. If there is any confusion, classification helps to iron it out. Once that has been done, the remembering process also becomes simpler due to the logical, structured nature of the classification process.

We know today that when we use methods of classification, the brain does not take in the information in a linear manner as it would take in a list. It continuously sorts, selects. It branches out in huge networks of ideas, juggling and inter-linking incoming data with previously stored experiences. There is analysing, coding, criticising. In other words, the brain does not work like a ladder, in straight vertical lines, but more like a spreading, sprawling map. This stimulates the broader, creative process which is like an ever-widening pathway of imagination, inspiration, vision ... A scientific invention is the complex product of structured information (or classifications) led by the brain in several directions until they finally emerge as something wholly new.

Similarly, art — whether painting or sculpture or cartooning — is also based on a classification of all existing knowledge and experience, and the moulding of this into something new by the artist's imagination. An eye-oriented person will visualise not just one or two flowers that he has seen, but will select parts and colours and shapes from others in order to create his own vision of beauty — a new whole. The ear-oriented person has several melodies classified in his brain, and he picks and chooses from them to create his own symphony — again, a new whole. In short, from classification comes a new comprehension!

When does classification become clerical and stultifying? When the classification itself becomes the be-all and the end-all of the task rather than a user-friendly structure. When this happens, the reproductive or recall power becomes stronger, but the ability to analyse and create is minimised or shut down. The brain becomes too literal in its processing and the thinking mind stagnates. This is useful when, say, quoting a bye-law in its exactness is required. But the *application* of the law so as to further the ends of justice or injustice is a job undertaken by the thinking mind. In the matter of using judgement, keenness and critical analysis, the mind can work for either the good or the bad!

Which is why I emphasise that the motive behind developing a good memory must always be self-improvement and the betterment of life. The right motive itself creates the correct links for the imagination to hook on to.

Chapter : 10

YES, YOU CAN...

Stop misplacing your spectacles, the house keys, the remote control ...

Organise your space and free your mind

Live for today... and live today fully

TOOLS YOU'LL USE

Key-hooks, Phone-pads and Work-desk basics

'A place for everything ...'

Delegation

Slowdown tactics

Right brain-left brain synergy

AND YOU WILL...

Develop a mind that is more focused, less wayward, less 'absent-minded', more 'present-minded'!

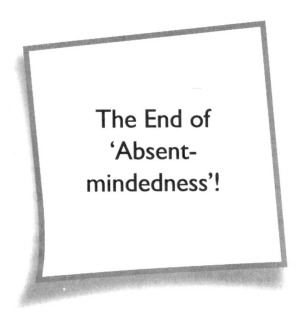

The End of 'Absent-mindedness'!

How to live in the 'present perfect'!

H ave you heard the one about... Gags about absent-minded professors (such as the one who stood in front of a mirror for two hours wondering where he'd seen himself before) are good for a laugh. But in real life, forget fulness and muddle-headedness can annoy and exasperate the people we live with, besides being a source of unending frustration to ourselves. In a recent popular poll conducted by the Saturday Times, 70 percent of the

women who wrote in groused that their husbands routinely misplaced glasses, keys and the TV remote control. One woman even reported, 'He invariably loses me!... The other day he dropped me off at the Victory Theatre and then waited endlessly at the West End to pick me up.' The men, on their part, 30 percent of them, also complained that their wives let the milk boil over, forgot to put sugar in the tea, and stood guilty of other sins of omission.

Sounds like a familiar strain? Do you find yourself groaning with regular monotony that you've misplaced your car keys, your house keys, an important document, a scribbled phone number? If so, you've probably spent long stretches of time looking for those elusive keys, documents and other items, getting yourself into a tizzy, a frenzy, and, finally, a panic about them. 'Why am I so absent-minded?' you wail, as you tear out your hair for the millionth time. 'Why can't I remember?'

The fact is, you don't have a poor memory; it's simply that you're poorly organised. Remember, you mind is like a file cabinet. If the files are poorly marked or out of order, you'll always find it difficult to locate something.

Fact no. 2: Chaos is not mandatory. There is a different way to do things. In a word, organisation! Organise your workplace and your home and you'll find you will free your mind. Here's how:

Clear out the Clutter

If your desk is strewn with papers, files and stationery like the rubble on Mumbai's roads, if you're holding on to shoes that hurt your feet because you can't bear to get rid of something you paid so much for, if your wardrobe has been in a state of overflow for years because you've been waiting for the return of the maxi, you're operating in an environment of material overload. And it's probably sending you through the roof. Each time you look at all that clutter, you feel overwhelmed, even depressed. There is too much of junk and untidiness around you, you get the feeling of too many things demanding your attention. Inevitably, this creates stress ... and stress undermines your ability to think clearly, setting the stage for memory lapses and difficulty in concentration.

In this kind of disorganised environment, not only will you find important items getting lost, but important information and chores also getting forgotten because your mind is so preoccupied with trivia.

The Solution. Throw out the unwanted stuff ruthlessly. Ask yourself (and answer honestly) the following questions:

Does it really serve a purpose? Will keeping it be helpful to me in any specific way? Am I ever actually going to wear this dress again?

Is it redundant? Do I already have another clipping that provides me with the same information? Do I really need to keep my old address book when I've already transferred these addresses to my hard disk and to a CD?

Is it quality stuff? How accurate and reliable is this tabloid report likely to be? Is it worth the space it's using up?

Can I access this information elsewhere quickly? If you have a CD that provides detailed and practical guidelines on emergency medical care, do you really need to have three books on first-aid measures on your shelves? Give at least two of them away!

Don't let your home become a greenhouse for junk — a place where everything comes in and nothing ever gets thrown away. When in doubt, clear it out — and you'll function with a clearer mind, too!

Have 'A Place for Everything and Everything in Its Place'.

This is one of the most life-enhancing adages that has come down to us through the generations. Many of us know where the 'important' things are kept — birth certificates, passports, income-tax returns, house deeds. It's the little, everyday things we can't find that are the chief time-stealers — the can-opener, the stapler, our sunglasses. But if you fix a place for each of those small things, remembering these places then becomes that much easier:

- Buying yourself a key-hook for keys is a good place to start. Alternatively, fix a key box just inside the front door. A friend of mine has a polished wooden key-hook shaped like a lock! She hangs it up just inside the door and pegs her house door keys and her car and garage keys on it. Other key-hooks — for her rooms, cupboards, suitcases, bank locker — are neatly lined up on another key-hook behind one of the most convenient doors.
  (While you're about it, make an extra set of house keys and keep them with a reliable neighbour.)
- Always keep a pen and writing pad by the side of your telephone. Secure the pen with a spiral loop to a hook near the instrument so that you don't 'absent-mindedly' carry it off and have to scramble around when you need to take down a telelphonic message.
- On your work-desk, make sure you've put in the basics: an in-tray for letters or documents that need to be answered or despatched. A box for pins and clips. A compartmented container for postage stamps, revenue stamps and international coupons. A holder for pens, pencils and highlighters.
- Keep separate files for electricity bills, telephone bills, guarantee cards, your medical history, rent bills. For investment certificates (shares, fixed deposits, bonds, mutual funds), buy one of those cellophane-paged files. Each certificate goes into a separate cellophane cover which makes for easy visibility when you thumb through it.

If you like collection informating (or need to do so for work purposes), keep a separate *Information* file. A friend of mine has a *Home* file in which she files brochures on home-improvement ideas, paints, electrical appliances, etcetera, which she picks up at exhibitions. Many of us also pick up such handouts at exhibitions but because we may not have a fixed place for them, we get ourselves into a flap when we need to find them.

Get into the Efficiency Habit

It's not enough to have a 'right place for the right thing'; it's equally important to make sure that everything gets into its place ... and gets there right away! If you've just got back home, *immediately* hang up your keys on the key-hook, *immediately* empty your purse or bag or briefcase and put your new purchases like postage stamps into their box, aspirin into the medicine cabinet, and so on. If you've picked up your mail on your way in to your office, put it immediately into the in-tray. If you've got out a fixed deposit certificate to refer to it, return it to its cover *immediately*. After you've paid your telephone bill, insert it *immediately* into its designated file. Do it *immediately*. Procrastination is what creates the clutter and the chaos.

Initially you may have to force yourself into the doing-things-immediately mode. But if you do it with a will and develop it into a habit, you'll find that very soon you'll be leading a more organised, hassle-free life. You won't be wasting half an hour looking for the Scotch tape. Since each item has been put straightaway into the place where it belongs, you'll *always* find it there when you need it. Your memory has filed away the information as, 'The Scotch tape is in the left-hand drawer of the work-table.' And when you need that tape, your memory produces the information in a nano-second so that you reach out for the left-hand drawer almost as a reflex action.

It's your organised lifestyle habits that have freed your mind of clutter, enabling it to always remember with precision and clarity.

Cure Yourself of 'Hurry Sickness'

Absent-mindedness often comes of a stressful lifestyle. By stress I don't mean just worries and tensions themselves, but the pace and mode in which you live. Do you jump out of bed every morning with thought of 'a-hundred-things-to-do' teeming in your mind? Do you rush through your morning cup of tea, or bustle about in such a preoccupied state that the tea grows cold before you can take your first sip? If the telephone or the doorbell rings, do you dump whatever you're doing and rush mindlessly to answer? Do you panic if *both* the telephone and the doorbell ring at the same time? Do you dash about from one place to another trying to get a million things done, in the process forgetting half of them?

If your answer is 'yes' to even one of these questions, you'll have found the cause of your absent-mindedness! At the frantic physical and mental pace at which you're living, you're bound to toss your keys hurriedly into some corner, tuck some important document into a magazine, place your spectacles near the wash-basin ...

Yet, you may wonder ... why the memory blackout? Is your brain functioning at such a sub-optimium level that it fails to absorb and file away where you tossed those keys?

It is not that you have a sieve for a brain: it is more a matter of how you are using your brain. The human brain has two different types

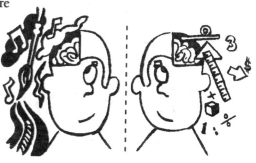

of consciousness. In the majority of people, the left brain deals with verbal skills (language), logic, numbers, sequence, linearity, analysis and physical movement. It is your academic- and motor-active side. The right brain is your creative side: it deals with rhythm, music, colour, images, imagination, face recognition.

When you live at a hurried, frenzied pace, you use only your left, motor-active brain, and it's in overdrive! But for a strong memory force, you need to use both sides of your brain. When you do that, there is a synergetic effect between the two sides via the corpos collosum — a network of nerve fibres that links the left and right sides of the brain. And your memory force needs synergy, not mere energy!

So, how do you live from both sides of the brain? By slowing down and allowing the corpos collosum to spark messages between the two sides of your brain.

That is why I urge you to live life at a measured pace, not as a so-little-time-so-much-to-do addict. Enjoy your cup of tea. Spend a minute putting away those keys in their designated place. Don't pick up the phone before the third ring. Whenever you find yourself about to rush off mindlessly somewhere, stop, take a deep breath and slowly count to 20.

Here are a few pointers on how you can put an end to

STOP! harried departures (the kind that have you rushing back home for the briefcase you forgot to take with you the first time you left home), an end to burning the candle at both ends, an end to having your meals on the run. In other words, how to take control of your time instead of allowing time- urgency to control you.

Don't Allow Yourself to Become One-Dimensional

If your life does not extend beyond the account books or project files, you are too uni-dimensional and you are stifling the synergetic process in your brain. Spread your wings. Awaken the child in you. You do that by doing the things that please your senses, not just the things that challenge your mind. Paint a shelf. Sew a quilt. Research your family tree. Do a crossword puzzle. Sing a song as you shower. You'll find that as your mind gets a breather from the world of words, numbers and ideas, your memory glows with a brighter spark.

Learn to Say 'No'

If your life is over-scheduled, it's probably because of tasks or commitments you shouldn't have taken on in the first place. Can you really give every Saturday morning to coaching the members of the Little Chess League if you've also committed every Saturday evening to choir practice *and* every Sunday morning to visiting the Home for the Aged? How many hours a week can you realistically spend commuting without turning into a nervous wreck?

Do you get the feeling of just not having enough time to finish the things you've started? And if you know full well that you've already got 20 commitments hanging and don't have the time for any more, whatever made you agree to undertake a collection drive for old clothes in the neighbourhood?

One way to work past your chronic inability to say 'no' is to resolve never to make a decision on the spur of the moment. With practice, it becomes painless to say, 'Let me check my schedule, think about it and get back to you.' So much easier on your time, your bunions and your equanimity than trying to keep to a commitment you never meant to in the first place.

Do not Strive for Perfection

That is the fast-tracker's trademark trait. Strive instead for accomplishment, for excellence. Leave perfection to those super heroes whose work you've been doing all this while.

A perfect example of the obsessive perfectionist is the housewife who works herself to the bone trying to maintain a 'perfectly clean house' — not a speck of lint or a mote of dust must be allowed to mar the antiseptic cleanliness of her dwelling. Such a homemaker generally has no time for recreation or relaxation. Unfortunately, she is also the one who almost inevitably ends up with not just frazzled nerves but also a snappish temper and ... repeated, disconcerting episodes of absent-mindedness!

Delegate, Delegate!

Do you faithfully keep the Eleventh Commandment: 'Thou shalt do it all thyself'? Control freaks have a problem delegating tasks since they are trapped by their own conviction that no one else can do a job as thoroughly well as they can. But you'll find (probably to your surprise) that if you delegate jobs and responsibilities, they do get successfully done. Neither corporations nor countries can run without delegation. Why should you?

Delegation means less unfinished business cluttering your mind. And that means a clearer mind, a mind that is more focused and less wayward ... less 'absent-minded'!

Live for Today

'One day at a time' is what being 'present-minded' is all about. Many of us spend so much time fretting about tomorrow's chores, next week's appointments, next year's increment, the next generation that we're raising, we tend to forget that the future we  plan and blueprint for begins *today*. When you obsess too much about tomorrow, you throw away today in mindless fretting and anxiety.

Instead, celebrate the present. Live it fully.

Workshop Extra

Make Writing Your Personal Aide

Isn't it strange? A single, extremely important idea flashes into your mind while you are busy with something else. It is so important, such a remarkable bit of inspiration, that you are positive you'll remember it later. But, when 'later' arrives, your mind is a blank. Yes, it was something 'important', but what in heavens was it? How often you find yourself feeling taken aback, puzzled, even shocked that that 'important' idea has slipped your memory so easily!

There are three reasons for this slip-up.

One is that at any given time you have innumerable thoughts and images jostling in your mind for your attention.

Two, the flash of inspiration was too brief to be imprinted firmly in your memory.

Three, you were not mentally relaxed at the time the idea came by so that it was pushed aside by another thought before it had time to register itself.

One way to avoid this kind of 'vanishing trick' is to quickly paint in your mind an exaggerated picture that incorporates the idea so that its absurdity returns to you. You can do this if you are in the shower or swimming. But you obviously can't do it if you're in the middle of a business meeting, for instance. Devising absurd-association images at such times is absurd and impractical!

The best way to make those impromptu ideas captive is to jot them down quickly. One of my friends who is a director on the boards of several companies, has made it a practice to scribble notes on the top right-hand corner of his sheets. After the

196

meeting, he says, he knows where to look for those flashes of inspiration. The top right-hand corner is his memory cue!

Jotting down ideas and other reminders to yourself is not 'sissy'. On the other hand, it shows that you *care* to remember, that you think something is important enough for you to note it down. Surely, somewhere you have noted down the numbers of your credit cards in case they get stolen. That's not being sissy, it's being sensible.

Writing down memos to yourself has three winning advantages:

1. The act of writing is personal, with your fingers guiding the pen across the paper. This personalised memo — of something you hear, or something that occurs to you — brings your sub-conscious into play. For this reason, sometimes just the act of writing down the reminder may be enough to enable you to remember it without having to refer to what you've written. Even if you don't, you can always recapture it by looking up your jottings.

2. Writing something down brings your visual power into play. What is visual power? When you've read something interesting in the newspaper and want to share it with your spouse, you'll say, 'It's on the front page, at the bottom right-hand corner.' See what I mean? You *know* where that particular report appeared. That is visual power. And it comes into play also when you write. You'll remember writing down 'something' in the left-hand corner of the page. That visual cue itself is often sufficient for you to remember *what* you've written.

3. Writing aids concentration as well. During those few minutes you are focusing on what you are writing, which

you are writing, which helps to store the information better in your memory. This is the reason that teachers, lecturers, professors, demonstrators write down certain key words or phrases. You hear them, but seeing them on the blackboard emphasises them and imprints them more effectively in your mind.

This is also the reason that students are encouraged to take notes. The notes are not only for memorising later, but also to make memorising easier by taking advantages of the benefits of writing.

The Best Ways to Take Notes

How do you take down notes? The best way is shorthand or one of its variations such as Shortrite. But if you do not know shorthand, there is another way. Let us undertake an exercise. Imagine that the great poet, Rabindranath Tagore, is delivering a lecture on his life. This is what he is saying:

'I was born in 1861: that is not an important date in history, but it belongs to a period of our history in Bengal. You do not know perhaps that we have our places of pilgrimage in those spots where the rivers meet in confluence, the rivers which to us are symbols of the spirit of life in nature, and which in their meeting present emblems of the meeting of spirits, the meeting of ideals. Just about the time I was born, the currents of three movements had met in the life of our country.

One of those movements was religious, introduced by a very great-hearted man of gigantic intelligence, Raja Ram Mohan Roy. It was revolutionary, for he tried to reopen the channel of spiritual life which had been obstructed for many years by the sands and debris of creeds that were formal and materialistic, fixed in external practices lacking spiritual significance.

There was a great fight between him and the orthodox who suspected every living idea that was dynamic. People who cling to an ancient past have their pride in the antiquity of their accumulations, in the sublimity of the time-honoured walls around them. They grow nervous and angry when some great spirit, some lover of truth breaks open their enclosure and floods it with the sunshine of thought and the breath of life. Ideas cause movement, and all movements forward they consider to be a menace against their warehouse security.

This was happening about the time I was born. I am proud to say that my father was one of the great leaders of that movement, a movement for whose sake he suffered ostracism and braved indignities. I was born in this atmosphere of the advent of new ideas, which at the same time were old, older than all the things that age was proud of.

There was a second movement, equally important. A certain great man, Bankim Chandra Chatterjee, who though much older than myself was my contemporary and lived long enough for me to see him, was the pioneer in the literary revolution which happened in Bengal about that time.

Our self-expression must find its freedom not only in spiritual ideas but in literary manifestations. But our literature had allowed its creative life to vanish. It lacked movement, and was fettered by a rhetoric rigid as death. This man was brave enough to go against the orthodoxy which believed in the security of tombstones and in that perfection which can only belong to the lifeless. He lifted the dead weight of ponderous forms from our language and with a touch of his magic wand aroused our literature from her age-long sleep. What a vision of beauty she revealed to us when she awoke in the fullness of her strength and grace.

There was yet another movement started about this time in my country which was called National. It was not fully political, but it began to give voice to the mind of our people trying to assert their own personality. It was a voice of indignation at the humiliation constantly heaped upon us by people who were not oriental, and who had, especially at that time, the habit of sharply dividing the human world into the good and the bad according to what was similar to their life and what was different.

This contemptuous spirit of separateness was perpetually hurting us and causing great damage to our world of culture. It generated in the young men of our country distrust of all things that had come to them as an inheritance from their past. The old Indian pictures and other works of art were laughed at by our students in imitation of the laughter of their European schoolmasters. The same spirit of rejection, born of utter ignorance, was cultivated in other departments of our culture. It was the result of the hypnotism exercised upon the minds of the younger generation by people who were loud of voice and strong of arm.

The spirit of revolt had just awakened when I was born, and some people were already trying to stem the tide. This movement had its leaders in my own family, in my brothers and cousins, and they stood up to save the people's mind from being insulted and ignored by the people themselves.

We have to find some basis that is universal, that is eternal, and we have to discover those things which have an everlasting value. The national movement was started to proclaim that we must be indiscriminate in our rejection of the past. This was not a reactionary movement but a revolutionary one, because it set out with a great courage to deny and to oppose all pride in mere borrowings.

These three movements were afoot, and in all three the members of my own family took active part. We were ostracised because of our heterodox opinions about religion and, therefore, we enjoyed the freedom of the outcaste. We had to build our own world with our own thoughts and energy of mind. We had to build it from the foundation, and therefore had to seek the foundation that was firm.

'As I say, I was born and brought up in an atmosphere of the confluence of three movements, all of which were revolutionary. I was born in a family which had to live its own life, which led me from my young days to seek guidance for my own self-expression in my own inner standard of judgement. The medium of expression doubtless was my mother tongue. But the language which belonged to the people had to be modulated according to the urging which I as an individual had'.

How would you jot down the important points in this lecture? Remember, the address is not laid out for you in print as it is now. Tagore is talking to you. You neither have the time to figure out what is important in what he is saying, nor can you anticipate what he is going to say. I'll demonstrate with the first two paragraphs how you should do it:

Born 1861,
History
Bengal,
Rivers, symbols, meeting,
spirits, ideals,
3 movements

Paragraph One: Born 1891. History. Bengal. Rivers, symbols, meeting, spirits, ideals. 3 movements.

Paragraph Two: Religious. Raja Rammohan Roy. Revolutionary. Reopen spiritual channels. Obstructed creeds. Fixed external practices.

What I've noted down above are key words and key phrases that will make sense when you later flesh them out into sentences. Regrettably, this method does not capture the beauty of Tagore's language. But for the purpose of remembering the substance of the language, poetic phrases are not only superfluous but can even impede recall. When you look at your jottings even a year later, you should be able to recall what Tagore said, not what you think he said. But if your notes are mainly made up of evocative words or phrases, over a period of time these words and phrases will have taken on a meaning for you quite different from what they conveyed in Tagore's address. This is because an evocative word is multi-faceted and its meaning for you is determined by your experiences and your emotions. So, at the stage of recall evocative words in your notes could conjure up images and ideas that are your own, not Tagore's. A key word or phrase should have a quality of permanence. When you write it down, it should imprint in your mind a specific image, and when, later, you read it in your notes, it should summon up in your mind the same specific image. This is what makes for accurate recall.

Note also that besides evocative words and phrases, you should also avoid conjunctions, prepositions and pronouns — in the interest of brevity and speed in taking down notes.

Now, I think you are quite clear on this. I suggest you practise with the remaining paragraphs of Tagore's lecture.

Keep Two Notepads. Here's Why...

Writing for remembering is particularly handy because most of us have two functional personalities: the personal and the professional. It's wisest to keep them apart. Bosses can be tetchy about employees who chat about their personal lives during office hours. And your family, likewise, might not be very enthusiastic about listening to your narration of office politics!

That is why it is wise to have portable notepads, a personal one and a professional one. Ideas and thoughts can then be separately jotted down to be followed up by the appropriate personality at the appropriate time.

Lee Iacocca, renowned for his management skills, lists out first thing in the morning, in an organised manner, all the things he needs to accomplish during that day. By the time he quits his desk in the evening, he has scored them all off! His slogan: 'If you care, you remember.' In practice, it comes down to: 'If you care, you remember, and you note it down.'

Ideas do not take a by-your-leave before they pop into your mind; they are no respecters of time or place. A writer-friend of mine said it took her years to figure out that those brilliant ideas that flashed through her mind when she was asleep somehow never saw the light of day. When she awoke in the morning, she knew she'd had an idea but she couldn't, for the life of her, imagine what it was. 'I'd comfort myself by saying, "Never mind, it will come back," ' she confesses. 'But not one of those ideas ever did.' This is a familiar experience and that being the case, I'd advise you to do what she now does: keep a notepad at your bedside. When inspiration strikes, harness that flash in a scribble!

At the end of the year, your notepads will also enable you to conduct a sort of annual review. You'll see what you've accomplished, which in itself will be gratifying. But equally importantly, your jottings will put things in perspective. This will help you avoid mistakes or superfluous tasks the next time round.

Self-conscious About Writing? Why?

Some people are self-conscious about writing in company. Take my word — there's nothing neurotic or obsessive about it, nor is it a practice that will diminish your image in any way. On the contrary, others will be impressed by your methodical habits (including the fact that you carry a notepad and pen), and even flattered that you consider what they are saying important enough to jot it down! In fact, you'll find several of them wistfully saying that they too should be cultivating this habit — though most of them never get down to it. Which only proves one thing — everybody wants a good memory, but everybody is not willing to work for it. In any case, why not enrich yourself? Why not jot down a delicious recipe, a good book title, the date and time of an interesting TV show? Why lose out on an inspiring thought, a poetic phrase or a brilliant idea?

However, if you do happen to be in a situation where it's simply too inappropriate to be writing down something, excuse yourself, saying you'd like to visit the cloakroom. Go to the bathroom and ... WRITE IT DOWN!

Chapter 11

YES, YOU CAN...

Deliver effective, polished oratory

Avoid blankouts

Overcome Stage-fright

Talk to, not down to, your audience

Motivate your audience to think, cooperate and act!

TOOLS YOU'LL USE

'The beginner's mind'

Reading with intelligence

Memory-fuelled inspiration

A speech plan

Delivery strategies

Confidence boosters

AND YOU WILL...

Use your mind, speak from your heart ... and reach out to your listeners' hearts!

A Good Memory Makes a Great Speaker!

....
'Mindful' steps to a memorable speech!
....

Reading the title of this chapter you might be led to conclude that I'm going to show you methods of memorising a speech. You couldn't be more wrong, my friends! Unless you are a trained actor, memorising a speech will only make you sound stilted or studied. You might just as well read out your speech! Instead, I'm going to offer you a few guidelines:

Don't Memorise Your Speech!

Never learn your speech by heart. If you do, you won't be communicating, that is, sharing your thoughts and feelings, but merely chanting out a string of words.

When you write out your speech as a preliminary to memorising it, you will be constructing it the way a writer does. And when you deliver it from memory, you will be sounding like you are reading out an essay — which in effect you will be doing. You won't sound like you are speaking *to* your listeners; you'll sound like you are reciting *at* them. Worse, you will be mentally occupied trying to recall your next line, as a result, your pauses will be not for effect but for groping.

Memorising your speech makes you extremely word-conscious, and that's exactly what enhances the danger of your mind blanking out. When he was due to address Parliament for the first time, Winston Churchill, one of the all-time greats in the Speakers' Hall of Fame, found that his mind had gone blank. Not a word could he summon up. His eyes gaped as the realisation hit him, he blubbered a bit and then he sat down, covered in confusion and mortification. He thought he had cooked his goose, that he was going to be a non-starter as a statesman. What had gone wrong? The man who was later to electrify the world with his 'Blood, Sweat and Tears' oratory *had memorised his first speech from beginning to end!*

Of course, he never repeated that mistake.

Do Put Your Memory to Work on Your Speech

I'll tell you what exactly this means — and what it *doesn't* mean. Many people think that preparing a speech is a kind of assembly job: pick up a few random ideas from here and there, a couple of quotes from the wise and famous, a sprinkling of dramatic phrases, a toss-in of clever sentences … memorise them to perfection … and hey, presto! You have a great speech in your hands.

Wrong! Absolutely wrong! A great speech begins with focused thinking on the subject you have been invited to speak on, reading up on it, perhaps even discussing it with others who may be qualified to contribute direction or ideas to it. Think honestly, not cleverly. From such thinking will spring forth a stream of well-considered, mellow ideas. More thinking will help to develop and expand them.

This is the stage at which your memory comes to the aid of your speech. As you ponder the subject, you are putting your memory to work upon it ... picking out thoughts, opinions, convictions, ideas, feelings from your great mind-sky, based on your past experiences and learning. And from these memories will come the *original thinking* that is going to make your speech fresh and dynamic rather than the stale serving it would be if you merely strung together material you have begged, borrowed or stolen.

Remember, we live in the Infotech Age, a time of information overload, in fact. Your audience may already be well-stocked with information on the subject you are going to speak on. So, if you just trot out more information, they are likely to walk away feeling cheated. At the end of your speech, your audience should feel it has gained something new — a *new* insight, a *new* perspective. So, do not hesitate to put forth your *own* point of view, even to propose a plan of action if that is relevant. And from where does this insight, this proposal come? It is garnered from your memories and from the multiple associations that they trigger off. It is what we call wisdom. And wisdom is what distinguishes a great speaker from a good one.

To open your mind to these associative memories, you must be in a relaxed state. This state of relaxation is not the rest or sleep that diminishes fatigue. It is a state of dynamic peace. Emptied of conscious thoughts, your mind is virginal ground, what the Zen masters called 'the beginner's mind'. It is the springboard of vision, freshness, individuality, inspiration. All of these will add uniqueness and vitality to the speech you are preparing.

More insights will arrive as you read up on the subject. This does not mean just reading up a string of books, but *reading with intelligence*. Which means that each time something strikes you as you're reading, you associated it with something you already know. Your association gives it more meaning and depth. Again, you can make such associations with your own experiences and emotions only when your memory power is robust.

As you think, read and talk about the subject, ideas will start tumbling forth, gushing forth in fact. Write them down! Not necessarily as full sentences, but as key phrases or in point form. Striking quotations you come across will, of course, have to be jotted down verbatim. So too bits of thrilling or inspiring verse.

Allow your mind to soak up these thoughts, ideas and insights like a sponge. Dwell on them, wallow in them. Don't just *think* of what you've put down on paper, but *feel* it. Let it get into your bones, so to say, and become a living part of you.

It's a good idea at this stage to try and encapsulate the central idea or theme of your speech in one compact and memorable sentence. Jot it down and repeat it a few times so that it becomes imprinted in your psyche. When that happens, anything you come across or experience during your waking hours that relates to this theme gets added to your notes.

You'll find, of course, that you've put down many more ideas, bits of information, quotations, statistics than you're ever going to use in your speech. That's okay. Though you may not use them all, each scribble further channelises your thinking in the direction of your theme, nudges your memory along.

Now, distil the essence of what you've jotted down and organise these thoughts. That's your speech! Or, more precisely, your speech plan. So let's discuss how you can go about it.

Prepare a Speech Plan

Broadly, your speech plan should be based on this outline:

1. You must first catch the interest of your audience with a joke or a small but pointed anecdote.
2. You must win the confidence of your audience by projecting confidence yourself ... confidence but not arrogance. You can say how you were once misguided until there came a turning point...
3. You will then come to the body of your talk. You will state your facts, confident that you have an audience that is ready to listen because you have already got it on your side. If possible, you will add local interest or flavour because there's nothing like that to win the hearts of your audience.
4. Now you will sum up and re-state your theme — the one you've already put into that one small, unforgettable sentence. You will motivate your listeners to think about the new insight you are offering them, to identify with your proposal (if you have one), and to follow through on it.

   Perhaps, if it fits in, you can have a closing anecdote, something that allows you to sign off on a light but sincere note.
5. And now you will sit down. One of the worst mistakes a speaker can make is to go on speaking long after he has finished what he has to say.

Your speech plan will be available to you for reference in the form of notes rather than an essay-style write-up. It's a kind of midway point — somewhere between memorising the speech and delivering it extempore.

An alternative presentation plan is to do as the ancient Greeks did when they delivered a flawless three-hour oration: associate the speech with your own house. Think of the opening paragraphs as the front door and the entrance passageway, and the body of your speech as the living room, bedroom, kitchen, dining room, bathroom, in the natural order you'd walk through them. End up by associating your conclusion with your balcony.

Before you actually go on stage, practise delivering your speech to your family or friends, referring to your notes from time to time. You already know what you're going to be saying about each point or you wouldn't have jotted it down in the first place. Practising before a live audience will also help you check out the logic of your reasoning, check out whether you're too long-winded, whether your speech makes the impact you're seeking.

What if a live audience is unavailable? Practise delivering that speech to yourself. Look at your outline, take up each point and start talking to yourself about it. Talk with feeling, and you'll find the words flowing out, surging forth. Where are all those words coming from? From the storehouse of your memory, that granary of impressions, feelings and countless mind-pictures. And because they are sincere words, you won't have to grope for them. In fact, you're likely to be amazed at how easily you will deliver that speech to yourself! If you try it a second and then a third time, the words may not be the very same, but they'll communicate the same thoughts and feelings. And you'll be getting closer and closer to a polished speech!

Don't Worry About Nervousness

Remember that all speakers, no matter how polished and experienced, and no matter how much apparent confidence they exude, feel nervous before they step on stage. Take a leaf out of their book: the best way to overcome nervousness is to *look* confident. The more nervous you're feeling inside, the more self-assuredly you must step up to the microphone. It works! Your body language will send positive messages to your mind and your nervous energy will transform itself into enthusiasm.

(In fact, the nervousness that precedes the delivery of a speech is a favourable sign because it is brought on by a rush of adrenalin as your body and mind prepare to take on the challenge of squaring off at a podium before an expectant audience. As you begin your speech, this same adrenalin will inject pep and punch into what you're saying. So, you see, what you really have to worry about is if you *don't* feel at all nervous as you step up to that mike!)

But nervousness is different from fear — or sheer panic. Fear is a negative emotion and it needs to be worked right out of your mind. It helps if you can fuel your mind with positive, self-enhancing messages instead. Think of it this way. Obviously, to those who have invited you, you are a person of some standing, or a specialist in the subject, or a thinker who will make his listeners think. So remember, as you step on stage and before the microphone your audience is literally and metaphorically looking up at and to you as a *somebody* — not a nobody. That fact itself is a great confidence-booster.

The knowledge that you've researched your subject well and that you can speak authoritatively on it is another confidence-booster.

As you begin your speech, you'll notice certain members of the audience looking at you with particularly attentive and friendly faces. Speak directly to them: you'll find that their unspoken endorsement will infuse you with greater self-assurance and that you'll reach out more easily to the rest of your audience.

In your delivery, use strong, simple language. Avoid bombastic pronouncements, transparent propaganda and anything else that your audience will recognise as sheer poppycock. If you speak from the heart — as you must — you won't need to sound clever. You will discover that the speeches which get the best response are the ones that simply say what you mean. That is all there is to effective communication. Simplicity and sincerity.

Do Look at Your Audience

Not memorising your speech has another advantage. You will be looking at your audience. And you will be able to see their reactions as your speech progresses. If you see them looking puzzled, you will be able to stop right there and clarify a point. If you find them looking enlightened, you will be even more inspired and every word you speak after that will carry a greater charge. If you find your listeners looking bored, you will know that you should change track or lighten up with an appropriate joke.

Do Trust Your Memory

If you've cultivated the right attitude of interest and if you've practised the methods of recall outlined in the earlier chapters of this book, your memory force will have been enhanced. And you can rest assured that your memory is a trustworthy fellow. If you trust your memory, you will be able to feel, and therefore project, more confidence and ease while delivering your speech.

Onstage, refer to your notes, take up each point and speak about it — just as you did when you practised at home. Think of it as a chat rather than a speech and you'll do just fine. You'll be talking *to* rather than talking *down* to your audience, you'll be using words naturally rather than for effect, and you'll be referring to your notes also as a natural process.

If you need to include statistics and figures in your speech, again know that you don't need to memorise them using the chain-association method. It's acceptable to read them out, raising your head every now and then to emphasise what you're saying as well as to gauge the audience reaction. Nobody expects you to be a memory-machine spewing out numbers.

But the chain-association method *will* help you when later you need to make a point *based* on the figures you've read out. You'll be able to *associate* the two and be more convincing because of your associative memory strength. This is one of the many ways in which a good memory will help you to think on your feet and thereby deliver a more effective speech.

Trust Your Memory's 'Reserve Power'

A novelist-friend of mine was invited by a women's Readers' Club. The subject for discussion was her novel, a story about a young girl who was burnt as a sati and is reborn. The author was asked, 'Do you believe in reincarnation?'

'Yes,' said my friend at once. 'But what I learnt from my

protagonist is that you don't need to be literally reborn. If you value life, you can experience several rebirths in the same lifetime. The scope is tremendous.'

At this, many of her listeners' eyes lit up, some heads nodded vigorously, some of the women seemed to focus inwards.

How would you describe their reaction? Enlightened. A surge of inner awareness. In effect: instant connection. The novelist had not trotted out various incidents of rebirth which, indeed, she had read about in the course of her research for the book. What she had done, instead, was to add *her wisdom* to the knowledge she had garnered on the subject.

And I'll tell you one thing more. My friend was not prepared to be called upon to give a speech. She had been told she was the chief guest, that it would be a discussion. When she arrived, she found she was scheduled to be introduced as the 'chief guest and main speaker'! She was naturally a little nervous at this discovery. But since she had worked so much on her subject, thought about it so much while writing her book, she found her memory force working for her as she spoke — extempore!

The most amazing thing is that my friend had *never* before given a speech, never entered an elocution contest or a debate. She is a writer who prefers to keep to herself. Any kind of publicity or promotion makes her tense and tighten up.

I think this is a classic example of how the memory force works for you. 'How did you manage?' I asked her.

'I didn't think of myself as the main speaker,' she replied. 'I looked at the expectant, friendly eyes around me. They seemed to feel I knew something they didn't. I told them frankly that I had not been aware that I was scheduled to speak and that I had not prepared any kind of speech. They didn't seem to mind. They said, "Tell us about your book and how you came to write it." So I began. After that, the words seemed to flow effortlessly!' She added, 'I guess it was easy because I'd got to

know the protagonist of my book so well that I could literally
see the world from her point of view. So, it was as if, were her
spokesperson appealing to everybody not to hold life so cheaply.'

I can explain why my normally reserved friend found it
so easy. She had read and collected a hundred times more
information than she could possibly use. And this information
had filtered down to her mindscape. When she needed it, it
was pushed to her consciousness by her memory force. This is
what Dale Carnegie calls the 'reserve power' that infuses colour,
vigour and, yes, wisdom into a speech.

So, as you see, there are no rules for successful speech-making
save this one: BE YOURSELF. Speak from the heart. Reach out to
your listeners' hearts. When you speak with your 'feeling mind',
your 'thinking mind' will follow. And your memory force will
be unstoppable!

Chapter : 12

YES, YOU CAN...

Challenge your brain to use more of its potential than it ever has before

Work mental muscles you may never have worked before

Actually alter the physical structure of your brain!

TOOLS YOU'LL USE

Brain teasers to race-walk your mind

Mental gymnastics

Rhyming cues

Abbreviation cues

New interests, new skills

AND YOU WILL...

'Outsmart' your brain and literally 'change it for the better'!

Memory Tricks and Treats

Fun ways to prompt recall!

Many people don't remember because they find it too tedious to memorise anything. This very often is a result of childhood conditioning. During their schooldays they were so bored out of their minds trying to memorise the multiplication tables, dates, formulae, state capitals, poems, that they now recoil at the thought of committing any facts to memory. In fact, my experience has brought me a valuable insight. Children who come from either an acutely unhappy background or from an extremely secure, balanced one, develop good memories. But those who grow up bored as a result of excessive wealth and luxury and pampering are the ones who have never been able to stoke what I call the Learning Emotion. Which is why I have decided to include this chapter of memory tricks and treats, I think Mnemosyne would have approved!

Who's Mnemosyne? She is the mythological Greek goddess of Memory! It's from her name that we get the word, 'mnemonics', which refers to the art and techniques of improving memory.

But let me assure you right at the beginning of this chapter that all the memory-improving tricks in it *are* treats! They are fun! Scientists are sold on them. Critics carp and say they are just another way of cramming your mind with more stuff than you really need. In my view, these critics are needlessly insulting our intelligence. After all, we are free to choose whatever information we want to memorise and to shrug off what we don't. In fact, their criticism surprises me, because developing a robust memory fuels your interest in the world of knowledge, in the people you encounter and interact with, in life itself ... and this enhanced interest in turn empowers your memory. It is a process of mutual back-scratching! And you are the richer for it.

The story of Stephen Powelson comes to my mind.

He was a Harvard graduate who worked as a company executive. One fine day, his firm shut down its European operations. And Powelson, at 60, found himself joining the ranks of the unemployed. Enforced retirement stared him in the face. But Powelson was not about to passively allow himself to become one of those retired folk who drift along, aimless and lonesome. To avoid this prospect, he knew, he had to keep his mind 'on its toes'. He wondered how he could best do this. One day, he idly plucked out his timeworn, college copy of Homer's

Iliad. Not the English translation, but the original Greek edition. Browsing through it, he was delighted to find that, so many years down the road, he still remembered the first 100 lines of the epic. So, Powelson set out to do something unusual. To memorise the entire epic — 24 books, containing 15,693 lines of verse! Just to give you an idea of how momentous a memorisation project this is, if you were to hold a reading session of the *Iliad*, it would take 18 hours of non-stop reading to go through the entire edition!

But Powelson memorised those 24 books. Sitting in his home in Versailles, France, he conquered the *Iliad*. It took him 10 years, but he did it!

Just think of an unemployed man finding such purpose in life, rising to such a stupendous challenge and emerging a winner! Patience, perseverance, interest ... Powelson had them all. Now, which critic would want to rob him of his victory?

If you had an elder sister or brother who helped you with your studies, you may already be familiar with some of those memorising tricks that students use to smoothen the rough passage of the academic years. In fact, reading this chapter will probably have you recalling facts and figures because you'll recognise the memory cues. Anyway here they are:

A Year's Calendar At Your Finger-tips: The Sunday Treat!

You can amaze your friends by telling them the precise day on which any date of the year falls! No, you don't have to learn a calendar by heart! Let's do it for the year 2000:

You just need to learn a 12-digit number to know all 365 days of the year! For 2000, the number is 265 274 263 753.

How did I get this number? Each number is the first Sunday of each month starting with January and ending with December. So it's like this:

JAN	FEB	MAR	APR	MAY	JUN
2	6	5	2	7	4

JUL	AUG	SEP	OCT	NOV	DEC
2	6	3	7	5	3

Say, your friend tells you to name the day on which August 25 falls.

Here's how you quickly do it:

The first Sunday in August is the 6th. So, the next Sunday will be the 13th, the next the 20th.

Add five days to Sunday the 20th and you get Friday the 25th.

Or, you can work it backwards. The first Sunday in August is the 6th. So the next Sunday will be the 13th, the next the 20th, the next the 27th. Work backwards two days and you get Friday the 25th!

So there you are. By memorising 12 numbers, you appear to your fascinated audience as if you have memorised all the 365 dates and days for the entire year!

Easy Verse for Recalling Dates: The Rhyming Treat!

If you have a problem remembering an important date, you can make up a rhyme with it for better recall. Like:

In nineteen hundred and forty-seven,
India became an independent heaven

or

In fourteen hundred and ninety-two,
Columbus sailed the ocean blue.

It's a great way to memorise dates. You can introduce your child to this fun method so that s/he won't be overwhelmed at the thought of remembering historical dates. All children love rhymes. And they enjoy making up their own!

Remembering The Right Spelling: The Letters Trick!

Many people have a problem spelling a word, particularly when the vowels, *i* and *e*, come together. The dilemma is: should it be *ie* or *ei* in that word? Here are some tricks to resolve the question:

> WON'T YOU HA
> A PIECE OF
> PIE ?

1. Is it piece or peice?
   It is p**ie**ce.
   Memory cue : A p**ie**ce of p**ie**!

2. It is niece or neice?

It is n**ie**ce.

Memory cue : A nice n**ie**ce.

3. It is cieling or ceiling?

It is c**ei**ling.

Memory cue : A celestial ceiling.

(Some teachers ask their students to learn the rhyme: '*i* before *e* except c.' But this is inaccurate. While, with this rhyme, they learn how to spell **ceiling**, they mis-spell seize, weird, leisure.)

4. Take **le**ave for **le**isure.

5. **We**ird is a **we**e bit crazy!

6. **Se**ize the **re**ins.

Use your imagination to create such memory cues and you will never again have to wonder whether it is *ie* or *ei*!

Abbreviations As Cues:
The Short-and-sweet Treat!

Almost every student uses abbreviations as quick cues. But this is only the second step in the remembering process. For example, you have to first memorise the names of the five Great Lakes in America — Huron, Ontario, Michigan, Erie, Superior. Once you know them, you can take the first alphabet of each lake's name and form a word out of them. For the five Great Lakes, you get a lovely, convenient word: HOMES.

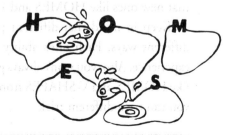

Huron	:	H
Ontario	:	O
Michigan	:	M
Erie	:	E
Superior	:	S

The bonus here is that you can remember the cue, HOMES, with *another* cue! Namely, that the five Great Lakes are HOMES for fish!

Similarly, first memorise India's seven mountain ranges: Vindhyas, Satpuras, Himalayas, Aravalis, Patkai, Eastern Ghats, Sahyadris. Next, take the first alphabet of each name and form a word out of them. For the seven mountain ranges, it is: V-SHAPES.

Vindhyas	:	V
Satpuras	:	S
Himalayas	:	H
Aravalis	:	A
Patkai	:	P
Eastern Ghats	:	E
Sahyadris	:	S

Once again, here, you get a picturesque second cue. That mountain ranges are inverted V-SHAPES!

This method is effective because we've grown up on initials as forms of abbreviation, the initials of a name, for example. Sometimes a person's first and second names have been abbreviated into initials and made into a nickname — JRD as in JRD Tata; JFK as in the popular sobriquet for Kennedy, and so on. Or, USA, UK ... If you notice, none of these initials form a word, yet they are locked into memory from constant use. It is because we already have this ability to remember abbreviations that new ones like HOMES and V-SHAPES come easy.

Keep in mind that different people remember things in different ways. Each one's ability will depend on his or her experience. Also, you won't always get convenient abbreviations like HOMES and V-SHAPES from the initials. In which case, you can try a different trick.

Sentence Formation: The Stand-in Trick!

I learnt a trick from a musician who had trouble remembering the lines on the music staff, the treble clef — EGBDF until a fellow-student gave him a simple sentence to memorise: **E**very **G**ood **B**oy **D**oes **F**ine.

E	:	Every
G	:	Good
B	:	Boy
D	:	Does
F	:	Fine

Here's one more which uses absurd association to remember the seven colours of the rainbow: **R**ichard **O**f **Y**ork **G**ained **B**attles **I**n **V**ain.

Richard	:	Red
Of	:	Orange
York	:	Yellow
Gained	:	Green
Battles	:	Blue
In	:	Indigo
Vain	:	Violet

Some have found the abbreviation, VIBGYOR, more convenient to remember the seven colours by. The question here is whether this abridgement is accurate and practical. Is the rainbow's uppermost arc violet or red? Here's where Richard's battle comes in handy! Of course, the best way to remember the colours of the arc is to reconstruct the visual picture from your understanding of science. You know that infra-red and ultra-violet are wave-lengths at either end of the colour spectrum. Now, use that knowledge to remember the sequence of the spectrum: red must pass through orange to become yellow, and so on. This is an example of how you use your memory intelligently.

Two Final Memory Tricks

Many people still have a hard time remembering how many days each month has. For them I recommend the childhood ditty:

Thirty days hath September,
    April, June and November.
All the rest have 31
    Except February which has one
more than 28 in a leap year!

Equally, I love the simple method I learnt when an elder sister was teaching her younger one. Close your fist and look at the knuckles. Every knuckle stands for a month with 31 days. Every hollow between the knuckles stands for February or a month with 30 days. Try it. You'll find yourself chanting as you touch the knuckles and the hollows: 'Peak: January; hollow: February; peak; March; hollow: April ...' and so on!

12,365 And finally, do you want to remember the height of Mount Fujiyama? It is 12,365 feet high — 12 months and 365 days in a year! Isn't that a wonderful association? How can you ever forget Fuji's height in feet after that?

IT'S A YEAR'S WORTH OF CLIMBING

Workshop Extra-I

Question-Answer Special

Over the years, I've been asked innumerable interesting, even provocative, questions about memory. It remains one of the biggest mysteries of the fascinating human mind. For instance, all the experiments in the words have not yet been able to figure out whether the laboratory rat has a similar or a different memory compared to a man's. A little progress has been made in the scientific investigation of this frontier of the mind, but much, much more is still plagued by big question marks. Nonetheless, I've compiled the posers that have been tossed at me most frequently, and tried to answer them as accurately as possible.

Q: Is it true that every bit of information we receive gets stored in our memory and that, if we only learn how to retrieve it, we can all be memory giants?

A: In a sense, yes. But there's a vital difference between the hard disk storage of a computer and the memory of a human being. A computer will *always* be able to give you the exact stored information. A human being's memory will not be so exact and unchanging. It is an evolving, creative faculty. A romantic, for instance, will look at the past through his regulation rose-tinted glasses. Even if he tries to describe it exactly as it was, his narration will be coloured by his perception. Distance will lend enchantment to his view.

Our memory is subjective and interpretative. In some ways, though, you can still call it 'loosely accurate'. Though I suspect that every stage of life has its own version of accuracy!

Q: But facts are facts. If we don't remember them accurately, doesn't that mean we have a poor memory?

A: Who is to judge the 'factual' aspect of the fact? For instance, if the romantic visits his childhood home after long years, he will find it in reality to be much smaller than he 'remembered' it. Or, a tree he thought of as a giant-sized specimen, would turn out to be pretty average in size. Which would you say is more accurate — his past memory or his present perception?

Q: How does a photographic memory work?

A: A photographic memory develops an ability called 'synthesia' — where the senses intermingle. Certain words trigger off colour and touch sensations. So do musical notes or sounds. Which means that the brain can turn anything into stirring, stimulating images that imprint themselves in the mind. Leonardo da Vinci was one such genius endowed with a photographic memory. He could sketch a detailed portrait of a person after seeing her or him just once!

Q: Is hypnotism a foolproof method for revealing truths hidden in our sub-conscious?

A: Hypnotism can be foolproof if the person being hypnotised is a willing and open-minded subject. For instance, in 1976 there was an incident in which a school bus carrying 28 children was hijacked. Under hypnosis the driver was able to 'remember' all but the last digit of the number plate of the hijackers' van. This enabled the police to identify and arrest the kidnappers and rescue 26 children. But had the driver been terrified out of his wits, the deep-rooted fear within him would have blocked his memory. This has been demonstrated in several experiments. People can lie or give a distorted version of the truth even under hypnosis!

Q: Should we always register a fact consciously for it to become a true memory?

WE SEEM TO HAVE OPERATED ON THE WRONG DISC...

A: Preferably, yes. But you never know what level of consciousness can store a memory! Many patients under anaesthesia are able to recall the entire conversation between the surgeons during the operation! Not unaided, but, again, under hypnosis.

Q: Is a good memory something one is born with?

A: I think we are all born with different levels of recall ability. But, ultimately, how well you remember depends on your desire and interest in doing so, and on how much effort you are willing to put into it. I knew an obese little boy who was the butt of everybody's jokes. He put on a cheerful, sporting front, but he worked hard at building up storehouse of general knowledge. Soon he had all kinds of information at his fingertips, including trivia! And people began to respect him. But earlier he hadn't shown any signs of being a memory giant. Unless we thoroughly know every person's childhood experiences, we shall never be able to really say whether some are born with the memory of geniuses.

Q: Is it true that we can remember things better in our sleep than when we're awake?

A: Though I do recommend sleeping over a problem to allow solutions to come through, I think staying awake is still the best way to remember something! No scientific research has yet shown that you can remember anything when you are in deep sleep. In a light sleep, *perhaps* — that's the premise on which subliminal tapes work. But the last word on those tapes is yet to be said!

Q: Why is it that older people can remember their childhood or youth so vividly, yet can't recall what they did last week? Doesn't this indicate that short-term memory declines with age?

A: This is the biggest memory myth I've ever come across! You'll never find seniors who are working or otherwise engaged in an interesting occupation exhibiting a 'poor' memory of last week! It's the lonely, world-weary ones, to whom last week is as dull and depressing as this week who can't recall recent happenings. The staleness, dreariness is what leads them into wistful recollections of brighter, youthful days — it's as if they are trying desperately to 'forget' the boredom of their present life.

Q: But, what about Alzheimer's disease? Doesn't that prove that memory deteriorates with age?

A: If that were so, every person who lives to a ripe old age would be struck by Alzheimer's. But this doesn't happen. It is not that a deteriorating memory brings on Alzheimer's, but that Alzheimer's affects the memory. Scientists know today that Alzheimer's is a specific organic condition that develops only in some human brains. It destroys brain cells and blocks communication between cells; in the process, it slowly but relentlessly erases a lifetime of memories. What brings it on and what makes some people vulnerable are only two of the innumerable questions about Alzheimer's that still await scientific answers. What we do know for sure: Alzheimer's is overwhelmingly a disease of very old age. Memory loss isn't!

Q: How much can a person remember over a lifetime?

A: How many stars are there in the sky?! But, one estimate holds it to be one quadrillion separate bits of information!

Workshop Extra-II

Exercises To Muscle Up Your Mind!

The assertion of neurologists that even the most creative among us use only about 10 per cent of our brains' potential is a troubling thought — as it should be. The good news is that we can do a lot to strengthen our mental powers. Psycho-biologists have found that the basis for 'smarter brains' is not so much the size of the brain or the number of brain cells per se, but the number of networks interlacing these cells. The more elaborate the network, the better the communication among the brain's cells, and the more efficiently the brain functions. And, the 'mind-blowing' discovery of intelligence research is this: *that we can increase the number of interweaving networks in our brains.* In other words, we can keep getting 'brainier'. It's in our hands!

How do we do this? By creating and living in an 'enriched environment', one that challenges our brains in new ways, extends our range of interests, expands our intellectual horizons. Such mental stimulation actually affects the physical structure of our brains, research has found! Now, isn't that an exhilarating discovery?

But how do you go about challenging your brain to scale greater heights? There are various routes: brain teasers, problem-solving, learning a new language, learning a new skill, reading a book on a subject you've never explored before. This Workshop brings you a sampling of brain exercises that challenge specific mental functions such as memory, logic and analysis, comprehension. Though each exercise is designed to test a different aspect of mental functioning, taken together the workout challenges and stretches 'the muscles of your mind' in the same way that physical exercise challenges and tones the muscles of your body. And as your mind responds to the challenge, your memory power will inevitably be enhanced.

There are 6 exercises in this Workshop. Before you begin each one, take several deep, rhythmic breaths; this will keep your mind in a relaxed yet alert state. Ensure you are in a noise-proof, interference-free environment so that you can bring the full focus of your concentration to bear on this exercise session.

Exercise # 1

Choose the word or phrase that is opposite in meaning to the numbered word:

1. Camaraderie
- distraction
- aristocratic
- friendship
- enmity

2. Fetid
- pleasant smell
- terrible smell
- thin and skeletal
- hot-tempered

3. Virago
- fierce
- saint
- highly talented
- fraud

4. Veto
- disagree violently
- underestimate
- agree
- beyond grief

5. Chimerical
- realistic
- surreal
- powerful
- acclaimed by peers

Exercise # 2

Choose the correct word from the brackets.

1. Your writing is (eligible, illegible).
2. She suffers from (aural, oral) pain.
3. The work-out cycle is (stationary, stationery).
4. His T-shirt is (loose, lose).
5. Every resident was present (except, accept) Rita.

Exercise # 3

Crack the code to get the words these letters stand in for:

1. CSBLF
2. BLJNCP
3. MJGFTUZMF
4. DOPTUBOUJOPQMF
5. SVCCFS XPPE

Exercise # 4

1. Add in the appropriate missing word: 'Tuesday is to Thursday, as Saturday is to _____'

2. Make a new word by adding to words below the correct alphabet from those given (no plurals and no proper nouns):

(i) sing (ii) win (iii) talk (iv) pain

Choose from: (i) T (ii) E (iii) T (iv) S

3. Re-arrange the jumbled alphabets to make works.

(Clue: Animals or Birds).

(i) EGOSO (ii) RGIET (iii) ACT (iv) KERAD

4. If July 1, 1998 is Wednesday, what is August 1, 1998?

5. My mother is the sister of your brother. How am I related to you?

Exercise # 5

1. If a=1, b=2, c=3, etc. what word does the following number make?

9451.

(a) Aunt (b) Bear (c) Idea (d) Fare.

2. If DQA means BOY, what does UKV mean?

3. Insert the single word that can precede all the three words below:

HORN   TREE   LACE

4. Fill in the three blanks using the same seven alphabets in the same order:

THE _____ WRITER WAS _____ _____

TO WRITE, BECAUSE HE HAD ____ _____.

5. What is the 16th alphabet?

Exercise # 6

Each scrambled word below describes a quality you need for a good memory. Unscramble the alphabets and find the words:

- STERNITE
- UMBIQUELIRI
- SENSEPON
- TRITENNACOONE
- MOSTIMIP
- NIMMETTOMC

Answers to Exercises

Exercise # 1

　1. (d)　　　2. (a)　　3. (b)　　　4. (c)　　　5. (a)

Exercise # 2

　1. illegible　2. aural　3. stationary　4. loose　5. except

Exercise # 3

　1. BRAKE　2. AKIMBO　　3. LIFESTYLE

　4. CONSTANTINOPLE　　5. RUBBER WOOD

Exercise # 4

　1. Monday

　2. (i) singe (ii) twin / wine (iii) stalk (iv) paint

　3. (i) goose (ii) tiger (iii) cat (iv) drake

　4. Saturday

　5. niece or nephew

Exercise # 5

　1. Idea　　　　　2. Sit　　　　　3. Shoe

　4. Notable; not able; no table　　5. P

Exercise # 6

　1. Interest　　2. Equilibrium　3. Openness

　4. Concentration　5. Optimism　6. Commitment

Besides these 6 specific exercises, there are other regular mental workouts you can do to get and keep your mind in top gear. Here are some examples. Once you get the idea, you can even devise your own on similar lines:

- Recite the alphabet backward from Z to A as quickly as you are able to.
- Say aloud the names of 20 parts of the body, numbering them as you go along. Thus, '1 — nose; 2 — mouth ...'
- Read at least one item in a section of the paper that you normally skip, say, the sports or the business pages.
- Work at a crossword puzzle or the *Jumble* word game.
- Take a walk along your regular route, but imagine you're doing it with a visitor to your city and that you're describing the place to him — you'll find yourself observing the landscape in a way you may never have before, even seeing things you had 'overlooked' before — such as the two *gul mohur* trees just past the bus-stop, the intricate latticework of a mosque ...
- Take a random word out of a book or newspaper, say, 'hit'. For the next five minutes, try to list as many words or phrases as you can that tie in with this word. For instance, *hard hit; hit it off; hit below the belt; hit upon; hit the nail on the head; hitman; hit out...*
- Take up volunteer work.
- Learn a new skill such as juggling balls, throwing a boomerang or eating with chopsticks.
- Try doing an everyday activity in a new way, say, drinking your tea with the cup held in the opposite hand, or sleeping on the opposite end of the bed.

No longer is it a foregone conclusion that your mental faculties will deteriorate as you age. The more you challenge your brain, the more you oblige it to work, the better your chances of staying alert and keeping or even creating an efficient memory.

Other Books by
Shakuntala Devi

150 puzzles are enjoyable exercises in reason, intended to sharpen your wits.

Match your wits with the 'Human Computer'
Shakuntala Devi
PUZZLES TO PUZZLE YOU

Shakuntala Devi
MORE PUZZLES
...to puzzle you!

300 puzzles, brain-teasers and mathematical riddles involving algebra, geometry and just plain straight thinking.

The international bestseller that woke the world up to the magic of numbers.

Shakuntala Devi
Figuring
The Joy of Numbers

IN THE WONDERLAND OF NUMBERS
Maths and Your Child

A fine way to introduce children to the concept of maths as fun activity.

Puzzles to Puzzle You (In Hindi)

शकुन्तला देवी
पज़ल्स टू पज़ल यू

SHAKUNTALA DEVI
AWAKEN the GENIUS in YOUR CHILD

The book will help parents combine the unique knowledge of their child's personality with the latest research on how children learn at each stage.

A complete book that leaves nothing to become an amateur astrologer.

SHAKUNTALA DEVI
ASTROLOGY FOR YOU

Shakuntala Devi
The Book of NUMBERS

Everything you wanted to know about numbers, but was difficult to understand.

www.orientpublishing.com

he'd told his Granddad to 'Piss off'. Mason had talked his Granddad off the ledge, assuring he'd get the information out of Mrs. Gale one way or another without Luke's help.

But he'd been unable to help Aeron. She slumped in the loveseat in their apartment, her hair a tangle and a far-off stare at the chessboard he couldn't interrupt.

"Decius, look at her," he said. "She hasn't eaten. I've barely got her to drink anything. And I haven't heard two words from her, except her screams when she finally sleeps. And she won't stop picking at the damned cut on her neck. There she goes again." He grabbed a tissue and moved next to her. She'd picked the scab off, and it began to bleed. He pressed the tissue to stem the bleeding and handed her a glass of water she wouldn't drink.

Lesley perched herself on the arm of the chair. "She'll be fine."

"I know she *will*," Luke muttered. "I just want to be able to do something."

"Aeron." Lesley swapped Aeron's glass of water for a mug of steaming liquid. "Drink this, please." Luke stepped back, letting Lesley take over, and could almost see the warmth of the mug seep into Aeron's fingers and up her arms. "It won't make you feel better, but it will make them." She nodded toward Luke and Decius.

Luke chewed his lip as Aeron's vision cleared with a few blinks. The mug moved to her lips. It was a small sip at first, but then she tipped the mug back and chugged. A grin found its way to Luke's face, and Lesley winked at them.

"Thanks." Aeron's voice scratched out, and Lesley nodded.

Decius moved beside him, and Luke didn't need to turn to know a foolish smile was on his face as well. They held their breath as she straightened up and looked around, finding Justin across from her consoling a haggard-looking Perry whose face was unshaven, clothes unkempt, and hair greasier than Arnold's Pick-Me-Up at the Diner. Luke would have to take him home, would have to piece him back together at some point.

"I have to get back home before the morning," Lesley said, gathering her few items.

Luke nodded. "Thank you."

"Really," Decius said. "You didn't have to come back here. You could have gone home."

Lesley gave them both a hug. "This is home. Any word on the status of training for us?"

Luke exhaled. His team had been spared at his request—they didn't know how far the Legacy had crumbled in the past few months, not even Decius. Word of Mr. Seward's betrayal and the fall of the Legacy made the rounds to those still alive, and they believed it was just a temporary hiatus. "You will be the first to know," Luke promised.

"Wait up. I'm going to go too." Justin sat up, leaving Perry holding on to consciousness enough to keep the bottle of Jack clenched in his fist. "If you need anything, let me know. Mason will know where to find me."

"What about Perry?" Decius asked.

Luke shrugged.

"I'll take him home," Decius said and pulled Luke into a half hug. Luke's entire body relaxed, the guilt, the rage, the regret melting away for a second. "I have business I need to take care of with your Granddad anyway. He's at the Mansion, right?"

"Yeah," Luke said, feeling the stress begin to build as Decius headed to the couch. He would tell him the truth, at least some of it, the next time they talked.

"Give me a hand," Decius said to Justin. They heaved Perry off the couch and half-dragged him to the door. Decius pried the bottle from his fingers and left it on the coffee table, and paused. "Take care of her." He nodded toward Aeron.

Luke nodded back as the door closed. Aeron's movement called his attention, and she wobbled, trying to stand. Her eyebrows furrowed in confusion, looking down at a heavily wrapped ankle.

"Whoa!" He rushed forward to stabilize her. "Take it easy. You wouldn't let us look at it after…I couldn't believe you were even walking on it, but Mrs. Gale said you were probably in shock." The cold crept into the back of his neck near his ear as Mrs. Gale's name passed his lips. Shannon's ghost trying to kill him from the grave, no doubt, for turning her mother over. He shivered, knowing he'd never be rid of their frozen gazes—and he didn't deserve to be.

"Is it broken?" Her voice cracked from lack of use and pink tinged her cheeks.

"No." He scooped her up and carried her to the couch, cradling her in his lap. "You'll be fine in a few weeks."

She shifted her weight, and fire burned in his leg from Rosemary's parting gift. He let out an involuntary hiss of pain.

"Your thigh!" Aeron tried to jump up, but he swallowed back the pain and held fast to her. He'd take a throbbing bullet wound any day if it meant the two of them alone and safe. "You were shot. Are you okay?"

"It wasn't as bad as it looked," he lied.

Aeron ran her hand along his thigh. Sparks jutted from her every touch. He closed his eyes and held back a groan the further up his thigh she went.

"How did this happen?" she asked, laying her head on his chest. "Luke—what happened on the yacht?"

He stiffened, realizing too late she was gauging his reaction. He kept his eyes closed to avoid her knowing stare. "I don't know."

"Don't lie to me." She grabbed his chin, turning his face to look at her. He looked then into her eyes, the pain clear into her soul. "They knew you. And the one who sh—the one who shot Shannon. We saw him before, trying to break into the apartment, and I met him that first week home."

He kept quiet.

"If I am leaving my Legacy and my brother to be with you, I deserve to know the truth."

"I *will* tell you." He would have to. And he would have to tell

Decius too. He hoped they'd stick by him the way Mrs. Gale stuck by Mr. Seward. But there was no way to know. So for now—for now, he could enjoy this victory: Aeron, alive and safe from her father. "But not tonight, Aeron. Right now, I just want to be here with you."

45

AERON

*A*eron placed her father's ashes in a stone urn, unmarked next to their mother's headstone. Decius refused to let him be buried on the property, or come down at all, so she sat beside the grave until nightfall, imagining what kinds of conversation they would be having in the afterlife.

Someone filled a seat beside her. She turned, expecting Luke— but Ivan had sneaked onto the property. His broken expression seared in her brain. She looked away.

"Why?" His single word held so much weight.

"Because he asked me to." She could have said no. That thought kept chasing itself around her mind.

Ivan scoffed. "He had no business being out of bed."

"What is that supposed to mean?" Aeron gave Ivan her best piercing look, and he held her stare.

"He had a heart attack two weeks ago. He shouldn't have been out of bed."

Her own heart seemed to fail her for a moment. "He...what? Why didn't you tell me?" He didn't answer her, but she knew why. To keep her focused on the task at hand. It explained how an intoxicated Luke had bested her father.

"Anything new from Mrs. Gale?"

He shook his head. "I haven't heard from her. Are you still leaving with him tomorrow?"

"Yes."

He handed her a thin file labeled Alexis Straganoff. "There's not much there. She came on the grid about three years ago, like the others I tracked down. Before that, she never existed." He paused. "I have to be honest with you, Aeron. Most of my surveillance shows her with Luke—and in more than just a work capacity." Her mind had become numb to tragic news, and she'd just nodded. "He killed your father, Aeron."

"No. I killed him, Darth." She shivered. She dreamed of killing him so many times—she never really wanted to, though.

"Technicalities. Luke's lied to you, over and over. He's known multiple times your life has been at risk and has never told you. You kil—" He took a steadying breath. "You killed your Dad instead of just telling Luke the truth. Now, I don't know what happened on that yacht, but can you be one hundred percent sure he had nothing to do with Shannon's death?"

She couldn't. Rosemary had been on the boat looking for information from him—she hadn't told that to anyone. She didn't know what it meant.

Ivan stood up, a cold breeze taking his place. "So tell me, Aeron. Is he still worth saving?"

She didn't answer him. But he had to be. There was too much blood in the water for him not to be worth it.

Aeron chewed on her knuckles, the countryside flying by as Luke sped toward the Wayward mansion.

"Are you alright?" Luke asked.

She nodded—another lie. She couldn't be further from alright. Her best friend died at the hand of one of Mr. Wayward's minions.

Her father died at her hand to make sure she could become one of Mr. Wayward's minions.

The Wayward estate loomed overhead; it never looked more uninviting. The weather reflected the stormy turmoil churning inside her, and the car pulled into the garage beneath the massive house. Luke opened the door and helped her out. Her eyes doubled. The garage was not a garage, but a showroom of cars, and one she'd only heard about through passing conversations with Luke's dad.

To one side sat an array of classic cars, including an Aqua 57' Chevy Bel Air and an Ebony '12 Ford Model T Speedster. On the opposite end of the room, she spied a midnight blue Jaguar, a Silver Audi R8, and an orange McLaren 570S. But the muscle cars against the back wall stole her heart. A gray '75 Dodge charger and a metallic sky blue '65 Shelby Cobra CSX 6000 roadster—which Ernie would have killed to get his hands on. The cars gleamed at her, warming her soul with each one she spotted.

A whistle escaped her. Her hand hovered just above the closest car: a royal blue 1930 Peugeot.

"This is beautiful." She moved between the cars toward a silver '67 Pontiac GTO, gazing inside. The keys rested on the seat. Her hands itched to pop open the hoods. "You think I could work on them?"

"That is something I'd love to see. They're neglected down here. Granddad doesn't have much patience for them. I'm sure he won't care."

"Do they run?"

"Um. I'm not sure." He looked behind him where a younger man with sandy hair stood cleaning tools. Aeron hadn't noticed him. "Hey, Kenny. Do these run?"

Kenny shook his head. "Only about half of them on that side of the room, Sir. The sports cars—all except the Audi run. Your Uncle Paul began taking it apart before his accident. It hasn't been touched since."

"Who works on the cars here?" Aeron asked.

"Just me and Max, ma'am. But we work mainly on the limos and the cars that are driven daily. These in here are left alone."

"Not for long," Aeron said softly, a small butterfly rising in her abdomen.

"C'mon," Luke said, gently tugging her arm. "We can come back later. Granddad is expecting us."

Mr. Wayward's office, like her father's, overlooked the family cemetery. Perhaps seeing all those lost souls was meant to be a reminder of what was at stake every day or where you ended up if you screwed up. She just saw loneliness and regret.

He sat at his desk in front of the large fireplace, and the firelight cast a shadow around, giving an ominous ambiance.

"Good afternoon, Aeron," Mr. Wayward said, standing when they entered. He walked around the desk and engulfed her in a hug. She stiffened, skin crawling beneath his touch.

"Thank you for having me," she said formally when he released her. She stepped back and couldn't stop her shocked expression. The scar she gave Ivan did not compare to Mr. Wayward's. Even though it had been over a month, the long marks looked only weeks old. He touched his cheek.

"Ah, yes. I've grown accustomed to it."

"What happened?" she whispered, blood pounding in her ears.

"An unfortunate incident that has yet to be remedied." His eyes flickered to Luke. "Now, for more current events. The business with your father was tragic. I hope we can move forward toward a brighter future for our Legacies." Luke pulled her close, and Aeron remained silent. "Feel free to make yourself at home here. The guest quarters have been made up for you. Luke, could I have a word?"

"Sure. Aeron, I'll meet you upstairs." He kissed her forehead.

Aeron left, dismissed by both of them. She headed up to Luke's room. It looked untouched. She used the opportunity to flip through the papers and books strewn around. She took a seat at his desk. In contrast to his messy room, the desk was pristine. A single notepad sat in the middle with a small container of pens off to the right, but nothing else.

Her hand shook slightly as it hovered over the first drawer.

"Are you going to open it?"

Aeron spun in the chair, her pulse racing. "Luke." He propped himself in the doorway, watching her. "What will I find if I do?"

"Nothing. It's empty."

Her hand dropped.

"What did your grandfather say?"

"That you can have free rein of the garages and to take your time settling in."

Her gut sunk. Not what she wanted. She wanted to be involved in planning, to be granted admittance to the inner circle. Anything. She moved toward him. He closed the door, meeting her halfway.

Luke's entire demeanor melted when the door clicked shut. The rough set to his shoulders that had developed over the past few months relaxed, and the softness of his brown eyes returned when he smiled at her—like the Luke she'd fallen in love with.

"What's on the agenda for the next few weeks? Do you have Legacy duties, or…"

"I have two glorious uninterrupted weeks with you. We can do whatever you want. We can go wherever you want." His eyes lit up with possibilities, and for a second, a millisecond, Aeron imagined them in Europe, the Caribbean, Japan. But while she indulged in a two-week vacation—people would be murdered. What if Decius was still on that list?

"Do you think we could lay low here?" She wrapped her arms around his waist and buried her face into his chest, the sweaty and musky smell intoxicating. He began drawing small circles on her back, the touch soothing and slightly sensual. Her skin shivered, aching for more of his touch.

"As long as we're together, I don't care where we are."

Aeron did not wait for Luke to instigate the kiss. She grabbed the back of his neck and pulled him in, capturing his lips with hers. Warmth blossomed in her chest, spreading throughout her body and chasing the dead from her mind.

Luke met her kiss with hunger, hands grabbing her waist, pulling her against him. The warmth in her chest began to pool between her thighs, every inch of her skin begging to be naked against him. Touching him. Tasting him. He broke the kiss, and she tried to recapture it, but he placed a kiss on her forehead.

"I love you, Aeron Seward," he said breathlessly, and she shivered in response. "I always have." His hands slid under her shirt, the heat from his fingertips shooting warmth straight to her groin, her knees unsure if they would hold her up.

"I love you." Aeron tugged at his tie, bringing him in for another kiss, her heart racing as his hands roamed her hips and bottom. Her skin felt electrified. Never had she experienced this kind of need. She wanted more. Needed more. She undid the first button of his shirt, grabbed the collar, and ripped the two sides away from each other. Buttons bounced off the floor, and she shoved the material from his shoulders. She lightly traced her fingers over his scars; most told a story they had written together. His body leaned into her touch.

His kisses became urgent, lips moving down her neck. Luke scooped her up, firm hands grabbing her bottom, and she wound her legs around him as they moved to the bed. He resumed his assault with feather-light kisses, starting with each finger and moving up her arm. Her body trembled, heart racing, and she licked her lips, savoring his touch. More. She needed more.

She reached down and ripped her shirt over her head, the cool air doing nothing against the heat of his touch on her skin, which left a trail of fire as his fingertips moved from her hips to her breasts. Her heart pounded, each beat driving her need for more of him. A moan left her, and Luke bit his lower lip, taking in every inch of her exposed body. Each scar, each bruise, he placed his lips. They traced a barely visible scar starting at the collar bone and inching down to the center of her chest. Her breath hitched, sensation building between her legs as he stopped at her bra. She undid her pants, wanting him to see all of her, but Luke's hand covered hers. She frowned at the loss of his lips on her skin, her body wanting nothing more than the burn against him.

"We can wait," he said.

"We've waited long enough."

He moved her hands above her head, and she left them there as his fingers traced down her arms. Her body arched into him as he cupped her breasts again, and he slid a hand underneath and unclipped her bra, her breasts falling free. He groaned as she tossed the black garment off. His hungry gaze sent a tremor straight to her core. No more waiting.

"Fuck me, Luke."

His eyes met hers, and he positioned himself between her thighs. Eyes still locked on hers, he grabbed the top of her jeans and slowly—so slowly Aeron thought the sensation alone would send her over the edge—pulled her pants off. She bit her lip as his hands moved back up her legs, her hips moving in anticipation. He moaned, pressing his erection into her leg. She moved her hips again, his reaction at her movement the sexiest thing she'd ever heard.

"I'm going to devour every inch of you."

He placed a kiss on her hip, sending jolts of pleasure between her thighs. He inched up her naked body, tongue tasting her skin, tracing a path from the front of her thigh to her stomach. Her body pushed into him again, and he smiled, pushing her back down. He was going to drive her insane with the excruciatingly slow touch— but she would love every torturous moment of it.

Her core tightened as he reached her chest, lips exploring every inch of them, except her nipples. Aeron grabbed his hand, placing it on her breast. He hitched a breath, rolling her nipples between his fingers, the sensation making every thought leave her head except one: she couldn't wait another moment.

She pulled him in for another taste, her body reached up, begging to be covered by his, and her stomach hit the cool metal of his belt. Her hands made quick work of his belt and pants, shoving them off. He helped, kicking the restraining clothes from around his legs and slid on top of her, the cool metal being replaced by his warm, hard member. She moaned, tilting her head back and wrapping her arms around his back as he repositioned to her entrance. She had waited an eternity and traded her soul for this—she intended to savor every moment of it.

Aeron bolted up, fending off invisible blows. She kicked at the bedsheets stuck to her sweat-drenched body. An arm wrapped around her. She gripped onto it and flipped off the bed. The body attached to it tumbled on top of her.

"Aeron!" Luke's firm hands halted her furious movements.

A scarred face faded from her nightmare. She blinked a few times, and Luke's bedroom came into focus.

"Are you okay?" Concern tinted his soft voice.

It took her a few moments to remember what woke her. Flashes of her father and Mr. Wayward flittered out of her consciousness, leaving only intense fear in her heart.

"Ron."

"I'm okay," she said, her heart pounding in her ears. "I'm okay." He lifted her up as the cool air nipped at her sweat-drenched skin. Forcing her hair from her face, she sat down on the edge of the bed.

"You're not okay." He paced back and forth, hand rubbing his hair. "This is the fifth night in a row you've woken like this," he waved a hand at her. He stopped pacing and placed his hands on his hips. "These aren't normal nightmares. Talk to me. Please."

Her eyes raked over his bare chest, following the map of scars. Scars—Mr. Wayward had starred in a few of her nightmares, but her father in more. The palm of her hand pressed against her forehead, trying to recall who visited her tonight.

"Aeron—"

"Shh. I'm thinking." But the memory skirted her probing thoughts and vanished. "Ugh. I lost it." The mattress sunk beneath Luke's weight, and he pulled her close.

"Have you talked to Dee?" he asked.

"No. He's still pissed at me."

"He'll come around," Luke assured. "He just needs time to wrap his head around everything."

She kept quiet. Decius couldn't understand why she never told him how dangerous their father had become. But he'd have to forgive her eventually. She rolled the tension in her shoulders and scooted away from Luke.

"I'm going to shower." His gaze burned into her back, but she refused to turn around.

The rhythmic sound of the shower hypnotized her, and she let the bathroom steam up for several minutes before undressing. She sucked in a breath, the scalding water pelting her, and sunk to the floor where the water was less intense. Tonight's nightmare might have escaped her, but last night's still haunted her: Her father assuring her they could save Luke and the Legacy and then running into her dagger. When he fell to the floor, Luke dropped too, his throat slashed. As she continued to turn, another and another and another fresh corpse dropped at her feet; Decius; Mrs. Gale; Ivan; Perry; Lesley. She couldn't stop turning, and the bodies kept falling. She took several deep breaths, willing the images to wash down the drain.

A knock at the door startled her, eyes flying open; she'd fallen asleep.

"Just a sec." Her voice sounded hoarse. She turned off the water, joints protesting the movements. She wrapped a towel around herself and pulled open the door, pushing the soaking wet hair out of her face.

Luke stepped back. "Hey." His eyes roamed over her body, and he bit his lower lip. "You didn't have to get out. I was just making sure you were still alive."

A smile crept onto her face. "I'm feeling better. What time is it?"

"Almost six."

Almost six? What time did they wake up this morning?

"How long was I asleep in the shower?" She tried to add some humor to her voice to mask her embarrassment.

"About an hour. Any longer, and I was going to break down the door." His smile did not breach the serious look in his eyes. Her gaze dropped to the suit he wore, and her gut twisted.

"What time are you leaving?" Even though he insisted he had two weeks off, Aeron knew he couldn't escape his Granddad or the Legacy for that long and didn't hold it against him.

His smile faltered. "In a few hours. I thought we could bring breakfast to the garage, and I could watch you work your magic."

She nodded, not trusting the words that might pour from her lips.

"I'll meet you down there," he said and dropped a kiss to her wet hair before leaving.

The room became too quiet with his absence. She ran to the drawer she'd taken over and grabbed some clothes. The rough material of the jeans pulled against her damp legs as she yanked them on, and the long sleeve shirt became wet where her hair hung against her back. She pulled her hair into a messy bun, her hands shaking as she flattened the overgrown undercut, and she clasped them in front of her. The blood in her veins buzzed with anxiety, and Aeron could not pinpoint where the sudden panic stemmed from.

Luke sat alive and well at the card table which Aeron insisted be brought down to the garage for eating. The racing in her veins slowed when her eyes confirmed he still breathed. Two large bowls of salad waited in front of him, and her stomach growled in response.

"This looks delicious." She dropped into the seat. "Where are you heading, and for how long?" she asked in-between bites.

He kept his eyes down, filling his mouth with food to avoid answering.

"I can come with you," she suggested. The fork stopped halfway to his mouth. "I mean…" But she meant exactly what she said, only Luke would never go for it.

He put his fork down and covered his mouth, rubbing a hand along his jawbone. Aeron stopped eating too. The carefree Luke of the past few days disappeared when he stepped into that stupid suit.

"Not yet," he said finally. "The dynamic of the Legacy has shifted in the last few months. I don't know if we will even have an Institute to go back to. I…" He looked out over the greasy car parts which littered the floor. "I don't think I've ever seen you more relaxed than you are in here. I'm not ready to give that up yet."

His words sent a flutter winding through her twisted gut. "What about you?" she asked. "It's been a long time since I saw you smile, and the second you put that stupid suit on, it's like you've donned an entirely different persona."

He moved the salad around on his plate, chewing his lower lip.

"I made some choices I can't take back, not that I would take all of them back, but I need to ride out the ramifications."

Aeron scoffed. "What does that even mean?" She tossed her fork down and crossed her arms. "I'm tired of being in the dark. I killed my father—me. If you don't trust me, why am I here?"

His mouth opened in surprise, and he paled slightly. It was the first time she mentioned her father to Luke since she drove the dagger through his heart.

"Forget it." Guilt gripped her. He couldn't tell her anything—Mr. Wayward didn't trust her. "It's a messy situation all around."

He took a bite of his food and changed subjects. "What are you working on today?"

She pushed the salad aside, no longer hungry, and rubbed her hands on her legs to warm them up. Her eyes scanned the garage, deciding which project would hold her attention until he returned home. "I'm thinking I'll start taking the engine apart on the Pontiac. That car is a gem if we can get it running." When she peeked over, his intense gaze on her sent a thrill through her core.

"Show me?" he said, raising an eyebrow at her.

He followed her toward the open hood. "So the carburetor sits here on the top." She pointed to the top of the greasy engine.

"What does it do?" he asked.

"It actuates the airflow into the engine, determining how much air is let into the airstream and therefore how much fuel is pulled into the engine."

"I'm not going to even pretend I know what you just said," he admitted. "How do you take it out?"

"Well, I'm actually going to take the entire engine out."

"Why?" He tilted his head, genuinely curious.

"Because it will be easier to clean and figure out what is shot and what can be salvaged."

"And how will you take it out all by yourself?"

"Slowly," she said. "Want to help me remove the hood?"

"Sure."

She tossed him a wrench. "Careful not to scratch the paint."

They worked in silence. The mechanical clicking sounds of the wrenches soothing Aeron. Once the hood sat safely to the side, Luke gave an almost-smile.

"What next?" he asked, eager to do more.

"I need to disconnect the battery, drain the fluids, and basically disconnect everything from the engine itself."

"That doesn't sound like fun at all." He sat down.

She laughed and returned to the car, making quick work of the battery and fluids. His gaze bore into her as she worked, and Aeron tried not to let the thoughts of him leaving sneak in. Moving to the radiator, she began working on the bolts holding the fan on. If she closed her eyes, she could almost imagine being at Ernie's, except for the unlikely combination of new tire smell and stagnant air. Luke's hands slid to her waist, and he peeked over her shoulder. She stopped working on releasing the fan and turned in his grasp.

They stayed for a few minutes, staring at each other, not saying anything while his thumbs made small circles on her hips. The inevitable buzzing in her bloodstream associated with his absences began in her legs, and she rested on the frame for support. He leaned down, capturing her lips for a brief kiss.

"Are you going to be okay?" he asked, his forehead still pressed to hers.

She nodded, knowing it was a lie.

"I'll be home before you know it. Don't do anything reckless."

"Like drown myself in the shower?" she said with a small chuckle. He cradled her face, lifting it to meet her eyes.

"I'm not worried about you drowning yourself. I'm worried about what keeps you from sleeping."

"They're just bad dreams, Lulu."

He dropped his hand and shook his head.

"What? Have I been talking in my sleep or something?" His weight shifted, but he didn't answer. She had been talking in her sleep. She shoved him. "Why didn't you say something!"

"I figured if you wanted to talk about it, you would." His voice rose a bit. "Plus, you never seem to remember what woke you, so why try and trigger the memories?"

She huffed and returned her attention to the Pontiac, twisting the wrench harder than necessary. What had she said? Which nightmares had her screaming out?

"Don't be like that." He encircled her waist and pulled her away from the car. She inhaled deeply, unable to stop the buzzing from working up her legs and into her arms. "He can't hurt you anymore. You made sure of that."

Aeron shook her head in annoyance. She wanted to tell him. She should just tell him. But she didn't have any proof here. She did at the Manor, though.

"Listen," he said. "If I could take that night back and how it happened, I would."

"You can't. It's a choice *I* made, and now *I* need to deal with ramifications," Aeron threw back at him. She leaned into him, though, and closed her eyes, Shannon smiling in her mind. "A pissed off brother and sleepless nights seems like a free pass. I could have been hunted for what I did."

"They'd never hunt you," he said into her hair. "I'll be back as soon as I can, but I won't be able to stay in touch." He placed a kiss on her head. "Keep yourself busy in here." She nodded beneath his chin, not sure if her voice would betray her words. "I'm sorry, I need to go."

"Don't be sorry. Just be safe." She turned, pressed her lips against his, and pushed him away. "Go. Before I chain you to one of these cars."

His fingers lingered on hers for a moment before he headed back to the main house. Aeron returned her attention to the engine, no longer interested in dismantling it. The anxiety in her veins intensified. She removed her phone from her pocket, rubbing her fingers back and forth over the raised buttons. Uncertain if Ivan would even take her call, she dialed.

He answered before the first ring finished.

"You okay?"

The concern in his voice floored her. "Yeah. I'm alright." Her voice betrayed the words, and Ivan knew it.

"Liar."

"Luke's heading to New York," she said, getting straight to the point. "I need eyes on him."

"Why don't you just go with him?" His annoyance hit her hard.

"It's not that simple, Darth."

"Neither is getting eyes on him."

"What about…" What about what? They'd lost all their surveillance when her dad went off the grid. And since the Gale house had gone up in flames before Mr. Wayward could raid it, she had no idea where Ivan or Mrs. Gale were. He could be in California for all she knew.

"Your brother took everything." The words sat heavy over the line. "You're still lying to him. He deserves to know, Aeron. Your Dad would want him to know."

The buzzing reached her ears. "Then he should have been more specific in what he wanted before he asked me to kill him."

"Aeron—"

"And if he really wanted Decius in the loop, he had plenty of chances to tell him. But you know why he didn't? Because—we are still on a growing hit list, in case you forgot. But his last request, Darth, was to save Luke. That is what I'm going to do." She stopped to catch her breath. "He trusted you. I trust you. Will you help me finish the job?"

The line remained quiet, and she checked the screen to make sure he hadn't hung up and waited for him to answer. It was like dealing with her father.

"I can't get eyes there," he said softly, and although she already knew he wouldn't be able to, his confirmation was a blow anyway.

She changed topics. "How's everyone fairing?"

His silence spoke volumes. The face of the Legacy remained upheld to the highest standards: essential connections maintained and backdoor dealings that kept the law out of their business. But on the inside, the Legacy was empty—on hiatus from all training and assignment—her father the patsy for it all. Mr. Wayward got exactly what he wanted.

"How's Mrs. G?"

"I haven't found her. I have no idea if she's dead or alive."

Aeron let out a long breath. Luke would have told her if something happened to Shannon's mom. She must be in the wind. "I'll end this, one way or another, Darth. I promise."

"It could be over if you came clean."

She shook her head but didn't answer.

"Stay safe, Aeron." He hung up, the disappointment in his tone straight from her father.

46

LUKE

*L*uke leaned against the wall opposite Interrogation Room 4. It'd been days of clandestine meetings with Dominic, errands for his Granddad, and a few deaths of the remaining Board members to round off his week. The only saving grace was there were no more kids to kill, and Rosemary was completely off the grid. Even Katherine hadn't heard from her.

The pristine white marble floors shone in the hideous fluorescent lighting, and Luke traced invisible circles on the floor with his foot, waiting for Mason to emerge. He shouldn't have left Aeron alone at the Mansion. It'd been only a few days, but his gut twisted at the thought of her fending off nightmares alone.

But Mrs. Gale hadn't said a word since they brought her in. It'd been over a week with no sleep, crumbs for sustenance, and dirty water. Add in spastic lights and music alternating in frequency, and it was regular torture training for Legacy members. Mrs. G still hadn't said a word.

The door opened. Luke caught a glimpse around Mason's legs, her eyes starring daggers at Luke, and a chill sped through him. She wasn't going to talk. The dark circles beneath Mason's eyes sent a tiny, almost minuscule feeling of guilt into his well-rested body. But Mason had promised results.

"She's not going to tell us anything we don't already know," Mason confirmed. He pushed the hair from his face and took post beside Luke, foot propping against the wall and giving a little bounce like he'd had too many coffees and his body needed to funnel the caffeine somewhere. "We will either have to move to physical persuasion or…"

Luke swallowed around the ball lodged in his throat. He'd hoped she'd just crack. See the error of her ways and spill the secrets his Granddad wanted. Luke didn't even know what secrets they were. "What do you think?"

Mason's half-hearted laugh echoed in the vast hallway. "Physical torture won't get us what we need. We're wasting time."

"That leaves just one option." Luke shivered as the thought passed to his lips. "Sin."

Mason shivered too. "Have you dosed it?"

Luke shook his head. He was supposed to have his first dose with Katherine and Perry at some point, but Rosemary's manipulating got in the way.

"I have."

Luke turned at the words. He didn't know the specifics of who needed to build a tolerance, but for some reason, Mason never crossed his mind. The light faded from Mason's bright exterior as the memory seemed to run through his head. Luke let him reminisce in silence.

"It's not something you forget. But it's especially effective after an emotional trauma. Eileen has taken it before too, but with Shannon's death so fresh, it might prove favorable." Mason's eyes met Luke's, clearer than the moment before. Whatever had him haunted passed. Luke wished his ghosts would leave him as easily. "It's up to you, boss."

He'd seen firsthand what Sin could do to an already unstable mind. The last time he'd watched an interrogation involving the neurotoxin, the man pulled out his own eyeballs, only to realize it was all in his head, and he couldn't stop seeing whatever haunted him so fiercely. Luke licked his lips. He'd probably pull his eyeballs out, too, if the demons and ghosts from his nightmares and daymares became a realistic fixture in his mind.

"What information does he want?" Luke asked. "Surely we can find less inhumane ways to retrieve it?"

"Were you still drunk when we brought her in?" Mason demanded, tilting his head and eyes narrowing. "You wanted to know why she kept him safe. *You* demanded her head on a platter. Your Granddad has already spoken with her and retrieved what was needed: the codes for the vaults that still stood in the rubble of the burned down estate. I could have put a bullet in her head days ago."

Ice burned by his ear. How could he have forgotten? Sleep deprivation and alcohol. On his parent's grave, he would not drink again.

"Does Aeron know you're torturing her best friend's mother for kicks? What the hell happened to you, Luke?" Mason shook his head. "I'm finished here. You want answers—you go get them." He brushed past Luke but paused by the stairwell. "Eileen is a great woman who has saved more lives than any of us. I don't take pleasure in what I've been asked to do, but I do it. Don't take my loyalty for granted again, Luke. Get your answers, and kill her yourself."

"Shit." He closed his eyes and dropped his head back against the wall, bouncing it a few times, letting the pain ripple through him. How had he forgotten?

After several deep breaths, Luke propelled himself forward, hand resting on the doorknob. Maybe he should go to the observation room first. No. He needed to see her.

The door knob slipped beneath his sweaty hand. He tightened his grip and waited for the retinal scanner to chime to push the door open. His nose scrunched in disgust, the urine and vomit odor leeching onto him in the darkened room. How had he not smelled it when Mason came out? His left hand found the light knob on the wall as the door clicked closed, and he turned it on slowly. A spotlight shone down over the heap of fabric in the center of the room.

He took a step closer. She'd been conscious and glaring not even five minutes ago; surely, she hadn't passed out already. He moved more swiftly, blood appearing to be seeping out from beneath the filthy garments. She couldn't be dead... the Monitors in the observation room would have sent a medic or hit the alarm at the very least.

The chime of the retinal scan registered in Luke's ear, and he spun. Mrs. Gale smiled from next to the open door. "I'm sorry, Lucas. It's for your own good."

"No!" He sprung forward, but her petite frame slipped through the small opening, and the door clicked behind her. "Damn it." How had she gotten out? Leaning in front of the retinal scanner, he waited for the lock to release. "Come on. Come on."

A buzzer sounded instead. "Unauthorized retinal scan," the feminine robotic voice said. He rubbed his eye and then opened it wider, trying again. The whirling laser scanned and buzzed again. "Unauthorized retinal scan," the robotic voice repeated.

"Damn it!" Luke's heart banged, and he pounded on the door, with just as much ferocity. "Mason! I swear, Mason, I'll..." He'd what? Luke stopped and slid to the ground, back against the door, and let his head drop back. He wasn't going to do anything because he was stuck in Interrogation Room 4, in an empty Institute, four-stories below ground, and had lost the last person on his hit-list.

He scanned the dark and disgusting room: the piss-pot strategically placed just out of reach of the chained handcuffs in the middle of the room, the spotlight hanging directly in the center masking the corners in darkness. Mrs. Gale would know those blind spots. She helped designed them.

He moved to the lump of blankets and clothing in the middle of the room. Depending on who they were interrogating, blankets were allowed. Sometimes to give a sense of comfort and home. Sometimes as a means to encourage suicide, with a metal pipe running overhead for ease of access. Not that they wanted them to die—yet. But bringing them back after they've attempted to kill themselves usually came with a spew of needed information, the will to live a bit stronger than before.

He pushed the blankets aside, the chain rattling beneath until he could see the metal cuff that secured around an ankle. It remained closed, blood and tissue caught on one side as if Mrs. Gale had forced her heel through the gap to get free. Maybe she had. Maybe she saw Luke and saw an opening. Or maybe Mason loosened it enough for minimal damage to occur. The small cup given for water was knocked over, now empty, but stained red from the inside. She'd probably filled it with enough blood to cause a distraction.

"DAMN IT!" he screamed. If anyone was in the observation room, they would have come by now. He needed to get out. The smell nauseated him, and possible ramifications for losing Mrs. Gale raced through his mind, all ending very easily with Aeron moving into Interrogation Room 5. Or worse, getting a dose of Sin while his Granddad manipulated the environment.

His hands moved to his pockets—his cellphone sat safe and sound. The Monitor's absence could be a good thing. He could call for help, and his Granddad could be none the wiser until he could track back down Mrs. Gale. His pulse quickened as options ran through his head. He scrolled through the phone until he landed on Decius. Well, now was as good a time as ever to bring him into the fold.

Luke waited with this back to the wall beside the door in complete darkness and out of sight of the screens if the Monitors came back.

The overwhelming stench of the room had faded, but the room's programing was still active. The soft buzz of lights warming up triggered a vice grip in Luke, memories of being in this room for training racing back to him.

He pinched his eyes closed, but the lights lit up his eyelids, so he buried them into his knees. The strangled cries came next through the speakers. Freezing sweat broke out over his body, Gabe's ever-presence pressed into him. With eyes pressed into his drawn-up knees and fingers stuffed in his ears, Luke hummed loudly and ran through the retrieval and handover of Mrs. Gale, racking his brain to produce the memory of demanding answers. He'd been hungover and sleep deprived, but he was pretty sure demanding torture was a memory worth cataloging.

The door swung open, brushing against Luke's tricep. Luke's fingers shot into the small opening, and he forced himself through the gap, rolling past a set of legs and into the hall to stand up. He reached past them and slammed the door closed.

Decius stared, hand still on the door, nose pulled up in disgust.

"Fancy meeting you here," Decius said, an eyebrow raised.

"Yeah," Luke replied, taking several deep breaths. "It's my secret hideout. Don't tell anyone." They both cracked a smile. Somehow even in this circumstance, Decius managed to calm the storm raging inside. The ice receded, the voices quieted. "Thanks for coming."

"Anytime. You know that." He stepped away from the door. "I don't need to know why you are locked in Interrogation Room 4, but I do need to know if we need to hightail it out of here or not. I brought the motorcycle, just in case."

"The motorcycle? It's been a while since we've ridden those." A foreign warmth crept through Luke's chest that reminded him of Aeron. They used to ride long nights for pleasure and fast nights for missions. "I have mine in the parking garage."

He shouldn't be thinking about riding through the countryside. He should be rushing back to Aeron, filling Decius in on…well, everything. And he needed to find Mrs. Gale. And Mason. But the glint in Decius' eyes that always promised mayhem and fun sparked something lost inside of Luke. He could enjoy one last ride with his best friend. Decius might not be so forgiving in a few hours.

"I'll race you to the mansion," Decius laughed, wrapping an arm around Luke's shoulder, and they raced up the stairwell.

47

AERON

The Wayward mansion had become a shell of what she remembered as a child. Dust collected in every room, spiders finding homes in the corners and underneath the beds. The only other occupants of the twenty-five-bedroom mansion were Perry, who must have buried his happiness in the bottom of a bottle and seemed to be drinking until he found it again, and his mom, Mrs. Wayward, who offered zero help in anything related to gathering information. She'd mastered the art of redirection and talked Aeron in circles until she forgot her original intention for starting up the conversation. Unable to stay in Luke's room for longer than a shower, Aeron spent her days becoming intimately familiar with cars Ernie would kill to be within spitting distance of.

Kenny and Max, the part-time mechanics, came in earlier, stayed later, and followed her around the garage like puppies. But between the cars and their company, the anxiety kept to a low buzz. They never had the guts to do more than wash the outside of the parked cars, but as Aeron continued to dig right into their guts, dismantling them where they sat, the two men asked endless questions and gave just as many useless suggestions.

She couldn't complain, though. The exteriors gleamed as if

showroom ready. Internally they were broken. Any repairs she classified as easy—a few fuses and new fluids—she let the guys handle. Other's required complete overhauls: such as rebuilding the engine and transmission. Kenny and Max weren't completely useless, but working with someone on a build required trust—and she didn't trust anyone at the moment.

Footsteps reached Aeron while she worked beneath the 67' Pontiac GTO.

"Kenny!" Aeron called. "What did the salvage yard say?"

"When I said free rein, I didn't expect you dismantle the entire collection of cars."

Aeron jumped. Her hand slipped and slammed into the transmission at Mr. Wayward's words. "Son of a bitch."

She stuck her bleeding knuckle in her mouth, and her heart pounded; what was he doing here? She took a few deep breaths before rolling the creeper out from under the car. She sat up and looked around. Mr. Wayward leaned against the wall, his feet crossed and arms folded. His silver-gray suit gleamed in contrast to the filthy area around him, and she focused on not staring at the scars on his face.

"I see you made yourself at home." His eyes roved over her grease-covered hands and stained clothing, and disgust clouded his features. A shiver raced down her spine, the similarity to her father unnerving.

She pulled out a rag from her pocket, wrapping her bleeding hand. "It's a shame to see such revered cars abandoned. I can have them reassembled by tomorrow. You won't even notice I touched them."

A smile flitted across his face. "Wait, you took these apart all by yourself?" She nodded. "I assumed Kenny and Max—"

"Those guys are barely experienced enough to change brakes, let alone take an engine out. Where did you find them—a high school auto-hobby shop?"

He laughed. "Close. These cars are useless to me. You could put them together with half the pieces missing, and I wouldn't know nor care. I'm here to discuss something else with you."

She tilted her head, doing a quick sweep for Luke, but they were alone. She rested her arms against her knees and looked up, interested in what he could possibly have to discuss with her.

"As you know, the Institute has all but been disbanded. We're working with a skeleton crew. Your father left quite the disaster behind him. I cannot thank you enough for helping us get rid of him. It must have been difficult."

Aeron dug her toes into the soles of her sneakers, willing all anger to funnel there to maintain a cool demeanor. "It had to be done."

"We're a lot alike, Aeron. We see what needs to be done and do it, even if it's a great loss to those around us. How is your brother fairing?"

She shook her head and shrugged her shoulders. "I haven't spoken to him much. Keeping busy." She waved her hand around her in case he missed her point. "What happens now?"

"That is up to you. I think you can agree the Legacy Laws have been unnecessarily cruel, especially to you, Aeron. Why should you be bound by a decision made centuries ago? So much has changed —the leaps and bounds made over just the past century have opened the door for progress. But the Laws, they hold us back."

"What is it you are suggesting, Mr. Wayward." Her pulse thrummed through her, and she wiggled her toes, relaxing the built-up tension. He wasn't wrong—the Laws were antiquated. That didn't justify killing hundreds of people, though.

"I'm offering you a home in a new organization. One that you voluntarily enter without committing anyone except yourself."

"And what about leaving?"

"Well, we all know you don't just *leave* this life, Ms. Seward. The organization is a work in progress."

She gave a short laugh. "So this is an offer between something new or death. What makes this new organization different from the Legacy?" She kept her voice steady, but her hands began to sweat.

"The Legacy grew greater than the founders ever anticipated, but their descendant's idea of grandeur fell horribly short. We don't belong training in secret amongst sub-par civilians and taking mid-level jobs. We are elite. Countries across the world pay top dollar for our skills. You make nothing with the Legacy. The money belongs to the Legacy and always returns to the Legacy. But what I am offering, Aeron, you will be paid for the work you do. You will get to choose the missions you take, not be ordered to kill against your morals—or even kill at all. We have positions for strictly gathering intel."

The deal seemed too good to refuse. How could so many Legacy families be dead then? "What about the rest of the Legacy? Is there a complete transition in the works?"

He didn't answer for a moment but pushed himself off the wall to stand closer to her, and she stood up, not wanting to be caught on the ground.

"I'm afraid there are many who did not see the proposition as appealing as others," he said. "You see, there are some new requirements and trainings. In order to dissolve the Legacy, all property needs to be liquidated back to the Blood families—and then, of course, the Blood families need to be in agreeance."

"And what of those who are not...in agreeance?" A cold fist gripped her gut. She already knew what happened to anyone who did not agree with Mr. Wayward.

"The transition is not optional."

"So, this is not an offer, but an ultimatum. Your way or the dead way."

He shook his head, a condescending smile on his face, which ignited the fire that had smoldered in the pit of her stomach for weeks. "So impervious for such a young woman. I'm offering—"

"Is that how Uncle John and Paul saw this—as an offering?" The words escaped her mouth before she could stop them. Mr. Wayward's lips thinned.

"Excuse me?" His voice held pure menace. She bit her lip, took a step back, and bumped into the car, a sick feeling that no matter what words came out of her mouth next, they were likely to be her last.

"I think it's odd—the biggest supporters of the Institute are all dead, and the program holding your ambitions back has collapsed. You've collected all that money from the decimated Legacy Families. Wilks told me what he was doing for you—he just thought you were keeping the money for yourself."

Mr. Wayward lunged. She grabbed the screwdriver tucked next to the engine and thrust it. He blocked it. She darted around him, barely getting out of his reach. She ran toward the dismantled cars, searching for a weapon and picked up a tire iron. His long legs caught up to her. She dropped low and aimed for his torso with the metal rod. He released a yell and doubled over. She kept moving.

Launching herself over the T-bird, glass shattered when she landed— a brake caliper bounced on the car's seat. Aeron brushed the glass out of her hair and moved toward the sports cars. If she could just get in one, she could be out of here. A shot rang out, and glass shattered to her left. She vaulted the Audi's hood and ducked behind the frame.

With only her dagger attached to her leg, her chances of survival dropped. His footsteps echoed through the room.

"What lies did your father fill your head with, child? Surely you have your doubts. I mean, you did kill the man."

Her heart pounded in her throat, her ankle aching in memory of their last encounter. But no one would be coming to save her this time. She looked beneath the car to gauge his distance—about fifteen feet. She grabbed a larger piece of glass and moved beneath the Audi, eyeing his progress. She slid out her dagger and waited. Mr. Wayward paused.

"We can be reasonable here."

He took a few more steps toward her hiding place. She tossed the glass toward the front fender. He moved forward, and Aeron rolled from beneath the car. She jumped to her feet and lunged forward, the dagger sinking into his thigh. He screamed and reached down. Aeron grabbed for the gun, knocking him to the ground. She held fast and twisted the weapon. It slid from his grasp, and she turned it on him.

"Are you supposed to be a Trojan Horse? You are a terrible one. You should have accepted my offer. We could've been on the way to D.C." He pulled the dagger from his leg.

Movement by the bay door caught her attention. She wouldn't be able to take on bodyguards, and she needed answers. "How many Legacy members have you killed, Mr. Wayward, not counting your own sons. Hundreds?"

"Does it matter?" he asked.

"Where is the Blood money going to?"

"A greater cause, Ms. Seward. You would have been a wonderful asset. Such fire in you."

"Shut-up. Did you really think you would get away with dismantling the entire Legacy?"

"I didn't think I would — I did. Don't you see? You are all that's left. You and your brother. Once I got rid of your father, there would be no one to oppose me — but you got rid of him for me."

Ringing had started in her ears. "Is that why you convinced Luke my father killed his parents?"

"It didn't take much." He laughed. "A few choice words, and the grieving son was ready to go."

A crash sounded, and Aeron whipped her head around, ready to fire. But Luke and Decius stood next to a fallen pile of tools. The sharp edge of her own weapon pressed against her throat, and her head slammed sideways, warm metal digging into her temple—Mr. Wayward taking advantage of her momentary lapse of judgment.

48

LUKE

"Granddad!" Luke yelled, his pulse thrumming through his body. Did he just hear that correctly?

His Granddad held Aeron in place, arm across her chest, the point of the dagger digging into her left shoulder, the gun kissing her temple.

Luke took it in, paling by the second. A single movement and Aeron would be dead, again.

"You see, Aeron, I knew you would be trouble, but you prove rather difficult to get rid of," his Granddad said, "just like your father." Luke took a step forward, and Aeron shrieked in pain, blood seeping down her chest.

"Stop!" Luke ordered, and his Granddad released the pressure, a sob leaving Aeron. "What are you doing?"

"I'm tying up loose ends, Luke. I—"

"Who killed my parents?" he interrupted. Because that was what they were talking about…his parents. His fingers wrapped around the worn grip of his Sig, and he lifted it. "Who killed them?" Decius moved beside him in solidarity, gun raised.

"I told you—"

"I'm asking Aeron," Luke clarified, ice coating the words as he readjusted his sight. The fire in his gut roared. She couldn't know… She wouldn't have let him believe…

Aeron hesitated, eyeing the gun pressed to her head and looking back at him. She wouldn't get a chance to talk before her brains painted the car beside them. "Let her go," Luke demanded.

"You're not in a position to make demands, son."

Luke fired a shot—the bullet grazed Aeron's side and lodged itself into his Granddad's leg near his femoral artery, but not quite rupturing it. Aeron slipped from his grasp and grabbed the dagger as he fell, kicking the gun from his hands. It skidded, and Luke kept her trained in his sights as she scrambled for it. She aimed the weapon back at Mr. Wayward before looking to Luke, her beautiful eyes widening as his sight remained on her.

"Whoa!" Decius pointed his weapon at Luke and took a few steps back.

Luke ignored them. "A neat trick, compliments of Rosemary," he said to his Granddad. "It's a beautiful shot that took many bodies to practice on. Now I need an answer." He looked at Aeron. "Who killed my parents."

She adjusted, her gun poised somewhere between him and his Granddad. "He did." She nodded her head toward his Granddad. "He's been lying to you." She pushed on her bleeding side with her free hand and grimaced. "He's the one who killed your parents."

The words echoed in his head. No. "No." Luke shook his head. "It was your father," he insisted, but the gun wavered in his hand, and he clenched it tighter. It *had* to be her father.

"What reason did he have to kill your parents? Where's the motive? They were *best friends* since…since forever! They vacationed together. Suffered tragedy together. They loved each other."

Luke's focus began to tremble, an ache in his chest threatening to rip out of him.

"She's lying, Luke," his Granddad said from the ground.

"SHUT UP!" Luke and Aeron's voices resounded in chorus.

"Your father killed your mother, and my parents knew," Luke said, retelling the story as he'd heard it. The narrative, which the only proof came from the files his Granddad gave him.

"She *was* killed—by him." She pointed to his Granddad, bleeding out. The growing pool of blood warmed Luke, but he shook his head, ignoring the urge to move closer to it. "They knew it. They tried to help my father prove it! What could possibly have surfaced to convince my dad to turn around after a lifetime of friendship and kill them in cold blood?"

"He abused you. He tried to kill you—"

"No. Our Senior Assassin tried to kill me," Aeron said. "That was me in The Rose Way. You didn't recognize the wounds?" Luke looked at the long scars on the older man's face. "I did it with the cuff you gave me. Even Katherine knew that. My father took the blame for my injuries to throw you off the trail—we needed physical proof."

What the hell did she know about Katherine? But he needed answers for the burning questions right now. "Proof of what?"

"Of everything. That he killed your parents, Luke, and your uncle. And that he has been killing hundreds of Legacy members; families, children." She paused, face pale as she caught her breath.

Luke lowered his gun, aware that Decius kept his raised. "Only the ones working with your father," Luke said. He ran a hand through his hair.

"No one was working with my dad. We were trying to save them, Luke."

"No." He refused to believe it. "He wanted the Legacy for himself—he wanted…" What did he want?

Aeron's heartless laugh assaulted him. "He wanted for this piece of trash to leave the Legacy alone. Your parents wanted the same thing. It's how they ended up dead. I guess it's easy to kill your own family when you have backups. Especially when you can use that anger as a catalyst for you to kill without asking too many questions." She took a few gulping breaths. "It would have gone perfectly if we didn't have feelings for each other."

"Feelings?!" His Granddad laughed, a hoarse wheeze escaping, drawing Luke's gaze down. "Does she even have feelings for you, Luke? Does she have feelings for anyone? She lied to you. How long have you known the truth about his parents? Since the funeral?"

The confession hung like an anvil in the air and toppled any reservations Luke had of his Granddad. Hatred and betrayal stirred beneath the surface, and he raised his gun again. Decius cocked his weapon. Luke glanced over. He'd forgotten he was even in the room.

"Put it down, Luke."

He shook his head. "How long have you known, Aeron?" He choked on the words as they escaped.

Tears filled her eyes, tugging at his heart. "Since the end of the summer. I wanted to tell you—"

"No. No—no." Flashes of innocent lives jarred into his head, some he had managed to bury, others who hung back like old friends, knowing he was wrong all along. He couldn't shake his head hard enough to be rid of them. "You let me work with this monster. You let me kill for him!"

"Let me explain!" she shouted. "I—was trying to keep you alive."

"Stop," he said, unable to drown out the buzz in his ears.

She kept going, though, "I just—I learned the truth about your parents, and I needed to keep you safe. I was afraid if he had even an idea you weren't one hundred percent on board with whatever he said, then he'd just dispose of you like he did his own children. I thought if we could find evidence on him, then we could take him down without hurting you. I swear."

"Does that include killing your own father?" his Granddad asked.

The words cut through Luke like a knife. All eyes turned to Aeron. He had nearly killed him—his parents' best friends. His best friend and girlfriend's father. She *had* killed her own blood. Luke couldn't imagine…

"He was already dying," Aeron said softly, eyes flicking to Decius. Luke looked too. Decius' devastated face seemed to crack Aeron's composure, and her gun began to shake.

"No," Luke spat. "All this time, you lied to me. You let me think he was a monster—I nearly killed him! And you *did* kill him. You killed your own father! Do you even understand how twisted that is? And all the while, you allowed me to train, and work, and live with that…" he aimed for his Granddad's forehead. He should pull the trigger. End this all here. He already killed so many—what would one more be? And the most guilty of all, at that.

"I'm sorry." Aeron's irrelevant words hung between them—the irreparable damage already done. He dropped his head, lowering the gun. He was done killing for his Granddad and for himself. He was done with everything. "Luke—"

"I don't want to hear it." He couldn't hear it. He'd done so much damage, and for what? "It's too late, Aeron."

A groan from the ground turned all heads to their Senior Assassin. A large pool of blood surrounded his leg, and his pallor was now grayish.

"What do you want to do with him?" Aeron looked at him. But he re-holstered his gun and turned his back, heading to the house. "Luke!"

"I don't care," he said over his shoulder, not stopping. Each step rocking his body, threatening to break the little composure he had. "Take him back to what's left of the Legacy and try him for murder, or put a bullet in his head."

"That right belongs to you." Decius, always the voice of reason and right.

Luke paused in his retreat and turned around, his eyes burning and blurry, his shoulders slumped. Decius had lowered his gun, and Aeron leaned against the fender of a blue car, now smeared with the blood seeping between her fingers. He wanted to run to her, hold her tight, tell her how much she'd saved him over the past year —but their lies—it destroyed them.

"Blood doesn't kill blood. Besides—he's already dying, isn't that what you're doing these days, Aeron?" He turned on his heel and walked away. The fire in his was gut gone, replaced by a cold so intense, he was sure he'd never be warm again.

"How many families are left, Mr. Wayward?" Aeron's voice sounded weary.

"None. Isn't that right, Luke?"

Luke's heart skipped several beats, the ice completely freezing him in place. Aeron's eyes bored into him.

The pathetic coughs sounded from the ground, the sound of a dying man. "You finished off the last four families yourself, son. I'd never been as proud of anyone. Your ruthlessness—" cough-cough — "legendary."

The ball in his chest ripped him open, and he stumbled, trying to catch his balance.

"Stop lying!" Aeron spat. "Your reign of terror ends today."

"I'm not lying. A dying man's confession is his most honest."

"Luke!" Decius called. Luke turned, the sins pouring past his internal walls and down his cheeks unchecked.

"Luke?" Aeron's face was a blurry sphere, but the disbelief in her voice was clear.

"I had to protect you. Your father…" he took a breath, realizing the real threat all along. "My Granddad."

"No. Lulu, tell me he's lying."

He couldn't.

"They—they were children. Babies! Literal fucking babies, Luke! Tell me he's lying!"

His Granddad had won. Aeron stared at him like the monster he was, and Decius, now next to Aeron, wouldn't even make eye contact. There would be no explaining. No pleading. No forgiving. It didn't matter how many he and Katherine had saved. Not to him, and not to Aeron. All that mattered was how many he didn't save.

"You're not going to finish the job, son?" The broken voice of his Granddad called across the garage.

"I'm not your fucking son." If he killed him... he would be no better than his Granddad. He'd only ever killed to keep Aeron safe.

"Fuck it," Aeron said and pulled the trigger.

49

AERON

The shot rocked her bones and echoed through the garage but found purchase between Mr. Wayard's eyes. Blood flowed freely from beneath his skull, and Aeron fought the urge to fire several more shots for good measure. But there weren't enough ounces of blood in his body to account for each death he'd caused. She looked back up to Luke, their gaze meeting for a brief moment before he turned and left the garage.

"C'mon." Decius tugged on her arm.

"What about the body?"

"I'll take care of it."

Aeron snapped her head around. Betty Wayward stood in the doorway.

"Mrs. Wayward—"

"Don't ever call me that again. I have dreamed of the day someone would kill that man. You two get out of here. I'll clean up this mess."

"Aunt Betty," Aeron said, the name bringing back childhood memories of running around on the Wayward grounds. "What about Perry and Luke?"

"You have just saved Perry's life, although I doubt he will notice much. And Luke—he's alive. Wasn't that your intention?" Aeron felt the shock plastered across her face. "I know an act of love when I see one. Get out of here."

Aeron glanced around the garage one final time. Broken glass glittered beneath the lights like a snowy day. She'd just become comfortable here.

"Thank you," Aeron said and didn't look back as she brushed past Decius toward the side entrance where they'd entered and saved her life, again.

She slowed down once outside, grasping onto her side, her breath hitching. Decius looked back. "Are you alright?"

She pulled her left arm against her chest, the adrenaline dying down allowing her muscles to register the searing pain in her shoulder from the blade." Yeah, just a flesh wound. Can we get out of here?"

He nodded and climbed onto the motorcycle parked in the driveway. It roared to life beneath him. Aeron pulled on her helmet and joined him. She wrapped her left arm around his torso, hissing as the shoulder screamed, and secured it in place with her right hand as he sped off the Wayward estate.

She closed her eyes, Luke's look of betrayal ingrained in her mind right beside Ivan's disappointment, Shannon's frozen look of horror, and her father's empty eyes. The cold wind bit at her silent tears as she tightened her grip around Decius, the pain from her shoulder and side tethering her in the moment.

There would be no fixing this. She couldn't change the lies she'd told or fix the countless lives she'd destroyed, all to save a single person. But Luke was alive—the whole reason she'd returned—yet he was far from saved. The Legacy was all but destroyed, and chaos would ensue. Rosemary…Legacy Inc… they would be out for blood.

And Luke would never forgive her, not that she could blame

him. She pressed her eyes closed, and his tear-stained face stared back at her. How many innocent lives had he taken due to her lies? Tears soaked the inside of her helmet, and she welcomed the suffocating feeling. They'd managed to keep Luke alive, but she wasn't sure they'd saved him.

50

LUKE

*T*he gunshot chased Luke through the house. He pulled out his phone, dialing Katherine.

"What is it?"

"He's dead." Luke's voice remained monotone. He should be elated or angry or anything, but he felt…nothing.

"What?"

"He's dead, and I'm done. Perry's at the bottom of a bottle, and I have no idea where your mother is. And I'm finished."

"Luke!" The panic in her voice kept him on the line. "We're not ready yet!"

"Not my problem."

"Luke—"

"Did you know?" Aeron's statement about Katherine flooding back to him.

"Know what?" Katherine asked, exasperated.

"That he killed my parents."

Silence answered him.

"Kat." It was more of a plea. He wanted her answer to be no.

"I had my suspicions."

"And you didn't think to share those with me? Stop me from killing all those kids?"

"They would have died anyway, Luke. We've been over this—"

"But not by me!" he yelled. "I could have… I might have…" He could have gone to Mr. Seward for help. Before D.C., he would have.

"And what of the kids you did save?"

What about them, he wanted to ask. All the ones who died— died for nothing. The ones alive, left alone for no reason. He'd lost his soul for lies. His insides were a battle of ice and heat, and he'd explode at any moment.

"They're alive," he managed to choke out. "And not my concern." He'd reached his bedroom. The comfort of the messy bed strangled him. Aeron never made the bed, and the first few days, it drove him insane, but it came to warm him. A reminder she was here, and safe, and now a lying, backstabbing…a furious scream escaped him, and every ounce of rage, and sadness, and frustration exploded from his body with it. How could Aeron lie to him? He only ever wanted to protect her. He loved her.

"Luke! Luke!"

Panting, he wiped at his face and picked up the phone that had fallen to the bed. "I'm done," he repeated, pure exhaustion swallowing him. "Mrs. Gale escaped," he warned, sniffing. "And Mason… I don't know where his loyalties lie, so good luck with him."

"What happened to you?" The words were so quiet he could have imagined them. But he couldn't tell her the truth: Aeron lied.

"I'm done," he repeated a final time and closed the phone. He tossed it on the bed and did a quick scan of the room. From every inch of shadow, the ghosts cried out. A chill chased down his spine, and he grabbed his jacket on the way out, returning to the garage.

Aunt Betty sat on the hood of a black Audi, her brown hair out of its normal bun cascaded down her back in loose curls, and her eyes locked on the lifeless body on the ground.

"He's really dead," she said when Luke came close. "All the damage that man caused, and he's finally gone." She looked up. "And you're leaving this mess behind."

"Did you know the truth too?" Luke's raspy voice clawed his throat.

"Which truth is that?" she asked in a parental tone he'd never appreciated before.

"That he killed everyone. My parents. Uncle Paul."

Her eyes widened. "He admitted it?" A dry laugh left her. "I suspected. He always loved his leverage." She slid off the car, skirting the blood on the ground to stand next to him. "I have been housebound far too long, cut off from the outside world. Perry's life was the only reason I didn't kill myself to be free of him."

"I'm sorry," Luke said, not sure why. She'd always been docile, quiet. He'd thought it her personality, but now he realized her spirit had been broken a long time ago.

"Don't apologize. I made my decisions. You should get going."

He looked around the garage, eyes skipping over the dead body. A single shot was all Aeron had administered, but he wanted to empty his clip into the corpse and then beat the crap out of it until he stopped having feeling in…in everywhere.

"You could go after her."

Luke shook his head and moved toward the door. "I can't. Even if I did understand why she lied, she will never understand why I…" The words wouldn't leave him.

"Then you should stay and fix the hell that's about to rain down on this family."

The responsible thing would be to stay. Technically, he was reigning Senior Assassin, now. The Underworld would be gunning for his head. The ball he'd kept under control the past few months expanded in his chest, his breathing coming in shorter bursts. He didn't want this. He wanted none of this.

"I—I need to leave." Without a backward glance, Luke rushed out of the garage to his motorcycle. Leaning forward on it, he took several deep breaths. Oxygen filled his lungs but didn't help his breathing. With shaking hands, he pulled on the helmet and turned over the engine, the loud exhaust drowning out the small voice in his head telling him not to go—reminding him of his oath to the Legacy and his team.

Katherine would never look at him the same, and he wasn't sure why he cared. Decius would never understand why he nearly killed Aeron. And Aeron…she'd never forgive him—that was clear in her horrified expression. Not that he could blame her. The weight of all the lives lost at his hand pressed down on him. But *she* was alive and well, and somehow, that almost justified it all…almost.

Luke revved the engine, a futile attempt to drown out his thoughts. The shaking in his arms was overtaken by vibration from the bike. He clicked into gear and sped off into the night. There would be hell to pay for his sins, by Legacy Inc., by the Underworld, by his own soul, but they would need to catch him first.

MORE TO COME...

Will Legacy Inc catch up to Luke? Can Aeron live with the damage she's caused? Is Katherine Wayward ready to step into her Grand-dad's shoes and run the most dangerous elite assassin agency in the world? See what killing the Senior Assassin without a plan will do to all of them in book two, The Assassin's Sin.

If you would like access to exclusive content and updates on the series, you can join my newsletter. And if you enjoyed this book please consider leaving a review to help other people fall in love with this world too!

ACKNOWLEDGMENTS

This book was in no way a solo effort. It has been the culmination of friends, family, and naysayers to bring it to fruition.

The biggest thank you goes to my husband, for your endless support and encouragement. This book would never exist without you. And to my children, who cannot understand the appreciation I have for their patience with me.

A huge thanks to all of the following for your help, support, and encouragement along this journey:

Mom and Dad, although you are no longer here to enjoy this milestone, you always supported me. Dad, I hope you are enjoying this final version!

My sisters, Moe, Julie, and Heather, you have been supportive since my very first writing days. Aunt Mary and Patti, you inhaled the very early, very underdeveloped versions of this masterpiece, I hope you enjoy! Beans—your excitement for this book was so inspiring, I couldn't wait to write more!

Alice Janell—for the inspiration, encouragement, silent writing sessions, and late-night meltdowns, but mostly for your friendship. Thank you! This book and this dream would have never made it without your help and badass VA skills.

Ms. Charlsie Russell, your encouragement in my early days fueled these rewrites and my ability to self-publish. Thank you!

The ladies who were in the trenches with me right up until the publication date: Taylor, Kristina, Kristine, Alice, and Shannon C.— You are amazing!

The ARC Readers who lovingly supported this first book. Thank you!

All my readers from the very beginning of this journey so many years ago, each of you had a part in making this book a reality! Deirdre, Sandra Dorr, E.G. Moore, Kadee, Amelia, Kelly, Isha, Brittany, Jen, Thalia, and so many, many more!

The staff of Martial Arts & More for the amazing hands-on training I've received to help create epic fight scenes, and the overall support of my goals. You are an incredible second family.

The agents who gave me positive feedback, and Mr. Stephen Morgan, who was kind enough to respond to my PitchWars entry with such enthusiasm and praise! It was the push I needed —Thank you!

To Michael Neeb, for bringing to life the audiobook!

To the staff of Salt and Sage Books for the professionalism and care they took with my book for developmental edits.

And lastly, to the TikTok Writing and Indie Author Community that are always unbelievably encouraging and supportive. You are some phenomenal humans.

ABOUT THE AUTHOR

After a childhood filled with James Bond marathons with her father, Libby brings to life a world of assassins and badass heroines.

When not writing, Libby spends her nights teaching self-defense and enjoying the art of jiu-jitsu. She loves English Breakfast tea, campfires, and loud music. She currently lives in North Carolina with her husband and two kids.

facebook.com/LibbyWebberAuthor

instagram.com/LibbyWebber_Author

tiktok.com/@libbywebberauthor

Made in United States
North Haven, CT
07 August 2023

40069048R00286